READY OR NOT

THE ART AND SCIENCE OF THE JOB SEARCH

WRITTEN AND EDITED BY

Justin Grossman

Doug Hanvey

Beth Kreitl

Katie Lloyd

Jan Van Dyke

CONTRIBUTING WRITERS

Laura Barnes Paley

Nick Podsiadlik

Career Development Center

Arts & Sciences Career Services

Indiana University Bloomington

Patrick Donahue, Director

Career Development Center
Arts & Sciences Career Services
Indiana University Bloomington
Patrick Donahue, Director

Visit our website at IUCareers.com.

This book was designed by Derek Springston.
The manuscript and layout was edited by Mary Spohn.
It was printed and bound by Metropolitan Printing Service
in Bloomington, Indiana.

The interior is printed on Weyerhaeuser's 70# Cougar Text Smooth, which is FSC certified and consists of 10% Post Consumer Waste. The cover is printed on Burgo's 100# Chorus Art Cover Silk, which is also FSC certified and consists of 50% Post Consumer Waste.

The text face is Sabon, designed by Jan Tschichold.

The headers are set in Akzidenz Grotesk, released by Berthold.

First Edition: June 2009
10 9 8 7 6 5 4 3 2 1

ISBN-10: 0-615-30284-X
ISBN-13: 978-0-615-30284-3

TABLE OF CONTENTS

INTRODUCTION

With few exceptions, we will all experience it—most of us several times. It can be a scary, time-consuming, exhausting, and frustrating process. We are presenting ourselves for judgment by others. We might ask ourselves questions like: What do they need to know about me? Will they like me? Will I fit in? Why haven't they contacted me? What if I never find one? What if I have chosen the wrong one?

The job search is, much like your life-long career journey, full of twists and turns into the unknown. You might feel ready for it; you might not. But regardless of whether you feel ready, if you're reading this, the job search is likely on the horizon—and you must get ready. The eight chapters that follow this introduction are designed to help you do just that.

Yes, the job search can be a daunting process, but it can also be a rewarding and energizing one if you allow it to be. It is an opportunity to better understand yourself and the world around you. It is a way to celebrate your strengths while recognizing and improving upon your weaknesses. And every transition to a new job or role allows you not only to appreciate all you have learned and the challenges you have overcome, but also to look forward to a "fresh" start and the acquisition of new skills and experiences.

An effective job search requires your commitment as well as emotional and mental stamina. Intentional scheduling of your time to dedicate to the job search is a necessity. The process is subjective in that each person will apply strategies in a unique manner. No matter your path, one crucial element is that you are consistently *active*.

But being active is not enough. Everything about the job search is subjective, and you need not be discouraged by this fact. A resume, cover letter, or interview question response that one employer finds acceptable—or even exemplary—may not resonate with a different employer. Likewise, the strategies you successfully employ in one job search may not work as well in your next search. It is nearly impossible to have a truly objective process when people are involved. Proper research can counteract some of the risks involved with the subjective nature of the job search—and this is why you will find the topic of research to be so integral to this text.

The strategies we discuss in this text have been designed to facilitate your job search process within the cultural context of the United States. Although other cultures may utilize comparable approaches, there will be nuances about which you will need to be informed in order to effectively navigate the job search process elsewhere. Additionally, there will be job search practices that are very different than those we have described here. As with all aspects of the search, research is vitally important.

You will see the phrase "job search" used regularly. When we use this term, we are writing primarily about the search for professional jobs and internships. So, when you read "job search" throughout this text, please remember that we mean both jobs and internships. We acknowledge that our textbook is not an exhaustive overview of all job search techniques; however, by using the research you do on each employer to customize your self-marketing strategies, you will have a strong foundation for the overall search process.

The job search process involves many stages. The first, essential step is engaging in self-reflection in order to clarify your work-related beliefs, values, interests, personality traits, and skills. Upon gaining insight into who you are, you will be ready to glean information about the world of work through career research. Confirming perceived interests and discovering and exploring new options will allow you to make an informed, conscious decision. After selecting your occupation of choice, you must effectively market yourself to employers through your resumes, cover letters, and job interviews. Understanding the critical pieces involved in successfully targeting your materials to a potential employer will help you set yourself apart from your competition. The job search process also involves understanding budgeting so that you are able to successfully negotiate your financial needs with the employer.

And here begins your transition from student to professional. As you launch your professional career, you are the ultimate authority on your destiny; it will be your responsibility to prioritize your professional development, to actively seek new and challenging opportunities, and ultimately, to manage your career.

On a final note, we want to draw your attention to the subtitle of the book: *The Art and Science of the Job Search.* Indeed, the job search is both an art and a science. The technical facets of executing a job search are related to the scientific process, in that there are logical steps to be followed and specific strategies to be applied. Understanding the "scientific" aspects of the search is critical to getting your job search off the ground. The "art" part of the job search has to do with understanding the nuances of how you present yourself, both in person and on paper. Simply stated, your job-search success depends upon your execution of the science; your opportunity will be affected by how artfully you approach it.

We enjoyed writing this textbook for you and hope you will employ many of the tools found within it as you embark upon your first job search, and as you change jobs or career paths in the future—whether you feel ready or not.

CHAPTER ONE

YOU

"People think that getting a job is the hard part: not so. Staying interested enough in the job to do it well and with enthusiasm is the real challenge."

– Howard Figler

INTRODUCTION

This book presents an organized and thorough introduction to the job search process, demystifying what you may believe to be an enigmatic and difficult process. But there is an initial step on the job search ladder that many people pass over in their hurry to get to the final interview—the step of self-exploration. As Howard Figler suggests, getting a job is one thing. Making sure that it will fit *you* is quite another.

If you have a job or career in mind, but don't know much about it, you should research it thoroughly (see CHAPTER 2). What are the tasks, the schedule, the salary, the future outlook? But this is only half of the picture. There is the work to be done, but there is also the person who will do it, the other half: *you*. Who are *you*? You can optimize the results of your job search by increasing your self-knowledge.

LEARNING OBJECTIVES

- Appreciate the importance of self-understanding

- Identify your work and job search beliefs

- Assess your values

- Be aware of your interest patterns

- Understand the fundamentals of personality type

- Be able to articulate your skills

You may think that you know yourself as well as you need to. You may even think that pursuing self-understanding is an unproductive use of your time; that it's best left to monks sitting in mountaintop caves. After all, from kindergarten through college, you've been habituated to the idea that knowledge of the world around you is the most important knowledge. But successful career development requires self-understanding, and the more the better. Knowing what you think about yourself and work (beliefs), what is important to you (values), what you like to do (interests), what makes you tick as a human being (personality), and what you're good at doing (skills), are all pieces of the "you" puzzle. Working on this puzzle will provide you with self-knowledge that will be invaluable as you define and pursue your career goals.

While self-exploration is a lifelong process, beginning *now* is well worth your time—if only to confirm that you're heading in the right direction. And because the majority of workers have more than one career in their lifetimes, increased self-knowledge will also come in handy in the future, when it's time for a change.

BELIEFS

A belief is a thought that we invest with emotional energy and hold to be true. A belief may be positive, such as "I'm a smart and capable person." But we may also hold negative beliefs such as "I'm not worthy of success." Whether positive or negative, our beliefs affect our perceptions of ourselves and the world around us, and influence the decisions we make and the actions we take.

Beliefs can help or hinder you in your job search. If you walk into an interview believing "I'm a smart and capable person," you're likely to have much better results than if you walk in believing "I'm not worthy of success." As Henry Ford put it, "Whether you think you can or can't, you're right."

To become aware of your beliefs, start paying attention to your "self-talk," the mostly involuntary thoughts that, for most of us, are constantly coursing through the mind. Paying attention to thoughts and the beliefs that underlie them may be difficult at first, but the more you do it, the easier it becomes.

For nine years—an unusually long time—the world record for running a mile held steady at just above four minutes. This led some people to believe that the four-minute mile was a barrier that would never be broken. In 1954, British athlete Roger Bannister ran a mile in 3 minutes, 59 seconds. It is said that in the following year, 37 runners broke 4 minutes, and 300 more did so the next year. Track experts never actually believed that 4 minutes was a physical barrier, but this story nevertheless illustrates the power of belief—once it was shown to be possible, many other people began to believe they could do it too, and they did.

Do you believe in your ability to find a job that you will like and your ability to succeed in it? Ask yourself if you hold any beliefs like these:

> *I will succeed in the job search.*
> *I will be able to get the job I want.*
> *I will start where I am, and get there one step at a time.*
> *I deserve to have satisfying work.*
> *My motivation and efforts will determine my success.*
> *I can have work that I like that is also practical.*

It's also important to check inside and see if you hold any beliefs that could undermine your job search, such as:

> *I will probably fail/I can't do this.*
> *There's no way I'll get that internship.*
> *Looking for a job is a painful process.*
> *I don't deserve to have satisfying work.*
> *I don't know where to start.*
> *It all comes down to luck.*
> *I have to choose between work I like and work that's practical.*

Once you gain clarity about your beliefs, you can work to intentionally cultivate the positive ones:

- *Affirm* a positive belief consciously by saying it silently or out loud to yourself, on a regular basis. Write your belief on a piece of paper and tape it to your mirror as a reminder, or create a screensaver for your computer that displays your positive beliefs.

- *Associate* positive beliefs with positive images and feelings. If you believe "I *can* get that internship," spend a few minutes each day imagining yourself at the internship, and allow yourself to feel the positive emotions associated with that experience.

While you're cultivating the positive, you can also work to release negative or limiting beliefs:

- *Consider* the origin of each negative belief. Is it really yours, or did you learn it from your parents, friends, or the media? If so, do you need to keep believing it? (For example, if you realize that part of you believes that "There's no way I'll get that internship," ask yourself the source. Do you have a friend who is so negative about the possibility of career success that you started to be negative too?)

- *Ask* yourself, do I really believe this is true, or is thinking this just a bad habit?

- *Question* the belief's validity. Ask yourself, is this *really* true? Can I really know it, for a fact? (Using the above example, you might ask, "Can I *really* know it's true that I won't get the internship? Can I predict the future, after all? How could I really know, anyway?")

- *Ask* yourself, what does this belief do for me? What do I get by believing this? (For example, you might discover that you hold onto that same belief because you're afraid that you might appear arrogant or too optimistic if you believed otherwise.)

The discipline of *cognitive-behavioral psychology* has developed numerous additional techniques you can use to change or release negative beliefs. You can learn about these techniques from relevant books or by working with a cognitive-behavioral specialist.

See Activities 1.1, 1.2, and 1.3 in the APPENDIX for written activities that will help you explore your beliefs.

THE BELIEF THAT WOULDN'T GO AWAY

Many of us have deeply held beliefs, which psychologists call *schemata*. We may not even be conscious of these beliefs, but unfortunately, that doesn't prevent them from causing us psychological pain and limitation. And ironically, they may be so central to our self-concept that we resist letting them go:

> *I'm an unworthy person.*
> *I don't have what it takes.*
> *The world is a dangerous place.*
> *I will never fit in.*

If you think such a core belief is holding you back in the job search process, or in life generally, working with a professional counselor or therapist who specializes in cognitive-behavioral techniques may be life-changing. Contact your university's mental health center for information.

VALUES

Your *values* are aspects of work that are important to you.

- A flexible schedule
- Doing work that helps others
- Upward mobility
- Lots of vacation time
- Working with people I like

These are just a few of many possible work values. Knowing your values helps answer the question "why do *this* work?" and is essential for opening the door to a satisfying career. In fact, people often leave a job or career because it doesn't satisfy one or more of their values.

While some of your values may change as your life roles and circumstances change, many may remain consistent over your entire life. Values are also personal, and the words we use to describe them may mean different things to us than to others. Take the value of "success." Many people want to achieve success, but what does "success" mean? One person might define it as making a million dollars. Another might define it in nonmonetary terms, as did magazine founder B.C. Forbes, who said that someone who "has done his level best ... is a success, even though the world may write him down as a failure." Or like anthropologist Margaret Mead, one could define success as "the contributions an individual makes to her or his fellow human beings." As you consider each of your values, especially abstractions like "success" or "purposeful work," consider what they uniquely mean to *you*.

RESOLVING VALUES CONFLICTS: *BRANDON FIGURES IT OUT*

Brandon was a recent college graduate who found an entry-level position as a part-time marketing assistant. After six months on the job, Brandon felt like a rubber band being stretched too thin. He valued having a "low stress" job, but another one of his values was to gain power and prestige by moving up in the ranks, which was going to involve hard, full-time work and some degree of stress.

Finally, Brandon had the epiphany that these two values were in conflict, so he decided to dig deeper. He asked himself *why* he wanted a "low stress" job, and *why* he wanted to gain power and prestige. What he discovered was this: He wanted to keep his work stress low because he had worked weekends at the family business throughout high school and college and felt like he deserved a break. He wanted power and prestige because he was always the "low man on the totem pole" in the same business. After realizing that these values were influenced by his experience at the family business, Brandon realized that moving up in the ranks was more important to him, and that he *was* willing to work hard again in order to do so.

When your values are in harmony within yourself, and there's a match between your values and the values you find in your work, you are much more likely to be satisfied!

Also, consider where your values come from. While some values are likely essential to *you*, others may be more superficial, unconsciously absorbed via interactions with family, peers, or the media. If Dad has always harped on the importance of a "secure" job, you may come to believe that security is among your foremost values. But after feeling stuck in that "totally secure" (and totally boring) job that you thought would make you happy, you might realize that "security" was really Dad's thing, not yours. Becoming aware of these influences now in order to discover *your* true values is well worth your time! (See Activities 1.4 and 1.5 in the APPENDIX for written activities that will help you explore your values.)

Once you know what your values are, what's next? You're in a great position to begin exploring the answer to the question: "Why do *this* work?" But there's one more step: You'll need to research potential careers that interest you in order to see if your values are reflected there. By matching your values to a potential job, you'll increase the likelihood that it will be meaningful and satisfying to you.

INTERESTS

An *interest* is something that offers satisfaction and enjoyment. Interests are often a strong predictor of the career choices that people make. Sadly though, there are many people who have never taken the time to consider what their interests are, let alone how to correlate them to a career. You've probably known people who didn't find their jobs interesting, and were often frustrated or depressed. Obviously, being clear about your interests is of paramount importance when it comes to finding work that you like!

John Holland, one of the most famous career theorists of all time, identified six broad categories of work interests. These six categories or "themes" describe occupational environments and one's work and personal interests. According to Holland, if you know your personal interest themes and discover a corresponding occupational environment, you're much more likely to be satisfied with your work. (See Activities 1.6, 1.7, and 1.8 in the APPENDIX for written activities that will help you explore your interests and interest themes.)

Finally, keep in mind that while some interests stay with us, others come and go. It can be helpful to reflect on your interests every few years. Career development is a lifelong process!

MEGAN'S INTERESTS: MYSTERY SOLVED

Megan had double majored in apparel merchandising and marketing, and had been on a steady track toward a career in retail management. While a student, she had worked her way up at a popular fashion outlet, and had also secured a summer internship at a trendy New York boutique after her junior year. But when she arrived for career advising only months before graduation, Megan was nearly in tears. She had gradually come to the conclusion that retail management wasn't for her. After exploring her interests, which included taking an assessment called the Strong Interest Inventory, and further discussion with her advisor, Megan realized that since she was very young, she had always been interested in the health-care field. She briefly considered continuing her undergraduate studies in order to prepare for medical school, but ultimately decided she would be satisfied with a shorter course of studies that would lead to a nursing license. Though she would not graduate as planned, her relief was evident. Getting clear about her interests was putting Megan on track toward a career she could get excited about!

PERSONALITY

Personality refers to a pattern of mental, emotional, physical, and behavioral characteristics of an individual. There are many theories about personality, but the most enduring and influential is Carl Jung's theory of "personality type." Jung believed that inborn mental tendencies tend to express themselves in regular patterns of behavior. People with similar tendencies tend to behave in similar ways, and thus are the same "personality type." Over a period of many decades, Jung's theory was developed further by the mother-daughter team of Katharine Briggs and Isabel Briggs Myers. Briggs and Myers developed an assessment, the Myers-Briggs Type Indicator (MBTI), to help individuals discover their personality type. The preferences that the MBTI identifies include:

- Where you get energy—do you prefer to focus on the external world of people and action, or your inner world of ideas and feelings?

- How you perceive information—do you prefer to focus on present realities, or future possibilities?

- How you make decisions—do you prefer to be guided by analytical reasoning, or personal values?
- How you deal with life—do you prefer being organized and methodical, or spontaneous and flexible?

As you might imagine, your personality preferences can tell you a great deal about the kinds of work you might like, or dislike. The four sets of preferences outlined above generate 16 unique personality types, and decades of research suggest that each type has specific preferences when it comes to occupational "fit." This rich and insightful data has made the MBTI the most widely used personality assessment in career development. If you'd like to make use of the MBTI for enhancing your self-understanding and career development, ask your university's career center if they offer it or other personality assessments.

SKILLS

A *skill* is an ability, based on training or experience, to do something well.

Skills fall into three broad categories. The first category consists of *transferable skills*, sometimes called soft skills. These skills are important in most occupations, so you can take or "transfer" them from job to job. Examples of transferable skills are communication, problem-solving, leadership, project management, and analytical skills.

The second category consists of *specialized knowledge*, sometimes called hard skills. Specialized knowledge is likely to be relevant to one specific job or career, but not others. For example, in the field of construction, the operation of a bulldozer requires specialized knowledge. In the field of graphic design, the ability to use Adobe Photoshop requires specialized knowledge. But if a graphic designer decides to call it quits and become a construction worker, her boss isn't likely to care that she's a wiz in Photoshop. Most occupations require some specialized knowledge. Sometimes an employer will provide the requisite training, but at other times you may need to possess specialized knowledge before applying.

The third category consists of self-management skills such as initiative, flexibility, and punctuality. From a learning perspective, these are not so much skills

TOP SKILLS AND PERSONAL ATTRIBUTES

In recent years, the following skills and personal attributes have been among those most often sought by employers:

- Communication skills

- Teamwork skills
  (works well with others)

- Motivation/Initiative

- Interpersonal skills
  (relates well to others)

- Strong work ethic

- Analytical skills

- Flexibility/Adaptability

- Computer skills

- Detail-oriented

- Organizational skills

as they are *personal attributes* that are relevant to the workplace. It's doubtful that someone can be trained, at least quickly, to be flexible or punctual, but that doesn't stop employers from seeking people with these qualities. It's well worth your time to consider what personal attributes you possess so you can articulate them as needed in application materials or interviews (see APPENDIX, Activity 1.9). Meanwhile, if you'd like to develop or improve upon certain attributes, you can begin the inner work that is required.

Identifying the skills you possess as well as the ones you like to use most (see APPENDIX, Activity 1.10) will help you to better match yourself to jobs, and especially to *satisfying* jobs. If you're going to be doing something 40 hours a week, you'll want to be using skills that you enjoy.

Finally, reflecting on how you've developed and utilized your top skills (see APPENDIX, Activity 1.11) will help you to communicate your value to potential employers.

CONCLUSION

Career-oriented self-knowledge will increase the likelihood of your job search success, as well as the likelihood that you'll be happy doing the work that you choose. Increased awareness of your beliefs about yourself and work will positively influence your decisions and actions. Assessing your work values will help you connect with the "why" of work—work that is meaningful and enjoyable for you. Clarifying your interests will help you find an occupation that is engaging and satisfying. Knowing your personality type will enable you to find valuable information about your own career preferences. Articulating your skills will help you communicate your value to potential employers.

Taken separately, these discrete parts of the "you" puzzle may each provide convincing arguments for a certain career path. But because the whole is often greater than the parts, you should also look for patterns and connections among your values, interests, personality, and skills. Such patterns will provide further confirmation of promising career directions.

Though you may have multiple jobs and careers that will satisfy you, as you continue to explore yourself more deeply, someday you may be fortunate enough to discover your *calling*, which is not necessarily a particular occupation or career, but the work which you were *meant* to do and that you feel you *must* do. When you discover your calling, you will find single-minded purpose, clarity, and passion in your work. May you discover your own calling, and in so doing, bring your deepest gifts into a world that is awaiting them.

CHAPTER SUMMARY AND KEY POINTS

- Successful career development requires self-understanding, and the more the better.

- Your beliefs, positive or negative, affect your perception of yourself and the world around you, and the success of your job search.

- Being aware of your values will help guide you toward meaningful work.

- Identifying your interests will enable you to discover the occupations and careers that are likely to be most engaging and satisfying for you.

- Assessing your personality type will provide valuable information about your natural career preferences.

- Effectively articulating your skills and achievements will help you communicate your value to potential employers.

CHAPTER TWO

RESEARCHING CAREERS

"Research is formalized curiosity. It is poking and prying with a purpose." – Zora Neale Hurston

INTRODUCTION

This chapter introduces resources available to you for researching careers, career trends, and potential employers. It also describes how to get experience in a career field of interest to you, as well as the process of making career decisions. Your career research will prepare you to find job leads in your field of interest, write stronger resumes and cover letters, and conduct targeted job interviews, which will be discussed later in this book.

CAREER RESEARCH RESOURCES

In order to give your job search direction, you should first complete the self-assessment process explained in CHAPTER 1. The self-assessment process will help you learn about your work values, interests, personality

LEARNING OBJECTIVES

- Understand the best resources for researching careers

- Identify trends in your career field

- Conduct effective employer research

- Understand the importance of trying out a career

- Use career research to help you make career decisions

style, and skills you enjoy using. After you have finished this process, you need to research career fields and job titles that relate to your self-assessment results before you are ready to look at specific job descriptions and announcements of job openings. Ask yourself these questions: Which jobs or careers match my values? Which jobs match the skills that I enjoy using? Which jobs match my interests and personality?

- A basic career resource to start with is the *Occupational Outlook Handbook,* which is a public document published by the U.S. Department of Labor. It is available online, or may be available in your school's career center. This resource gives thorough descriptions of hundreds of jobs. It includes details about each job, including salary, training and education needed, projected job growth, skills required, job advancement opportunities, and a description of the work environment.

- Another resource is the *Encyclopedia of Careers.* This book is similar to the *Occupational Outlook Handbook,* but includes information about additional jobs not covered in the handbook. Details for each job include: an overview and history of the job, earnings, requirements, and job outlook.

- *The Vocational Biographies* series is a collection of hundreds of informational interviews with people who talk about their jobs. The people who are interviewed speak about how they got started in their field and what they like and don't like about their jobs. This resource describes job activities, training, qualifications, and salary range. This information is very helpful as you decide whether a specific job or career field is a good fit for you.

In addition to these resources, your school's career center may have a variety of career exploration books. Examples of these books include: the Great Jobs series (e.g., *Great Jobs for Political Science Majors*) and the Careers For series (e.g., *Careers for Fashion Plates & Other Trendsetters*) and the Career Opportunities In series (e.g., *Career Opportunities in the Film Industry*). These career exploration books will help you get a better understanding of the career field and descriptions of the jobs within the career field. These books include information about education and training needed, job advancement opportunities, experience, skills, and personality traits desired for a specific career field.

Also check your school's career center website, which may include many additional resources and links to more career research websites.

The career research process will either reinforce or challenge your first impressions of your top career choices, and will provide valuable information for your job search. For each career you research, try to find the following information:

- Daily activities of the job

- Working conditions (Do you work inside or outside? Do you work in teams or by yourself? Will you be traveling? Do you have an office?)

- Potential places of employment

- Required education and training (Are special certifications required?)

- Personal characteristics (Does the employer prefer someone who is outgoing and high energy, or someone who is more reserved? Does the employer want someone who is flexible and adaptable, or someone who is more structured and orderly who pays strict attention to detail?)

- Salary

- Advancement opportunities

- Future job outlook (Is there an increase or decline, or steady job growth? How many jobs are being created in the career field of interest to you?)

- Specific job titles within the career field

Most people spend more time researching the car they want to purchase than they spend researching a potential career. For example, you can spend many hours researching your ideal car. You can research costs, fuel efficiency, safety features, and many other details. You should research your future career and job with the same sense of enthusiasm and attention to detail. Remember, you will be spending 40 or more hours a week at your job, so researching careers is time well spent.

In addition to reading about careers in books and on websites, it's a good idea to supplement what you have learned by talking to professionals in a career field of interest to you. This technique is called informational interviewing.

INFORMATIONAL INTERVIEWS

Book research is very important for career exploration, but no book or website can answer all of your questions. An informational interview with a person who works in a career field of interest to you can provide information about your career field's job requirements, future job outlook, and training that is required. Informational interviewing is different from a job or internship interview in that *you* are initiating the discussion, and therefore *you* are the interviewer. The person you interview can give you an insider's perspective of the career and give you the most current information about how the career field is changing. If you have done a good job of researching, you should have additional questions to ask during the informational interview. The person you are interviewing may be impressed that you took the time to research their job and career field. As a result of your research, you will have a much better informational interview.

PURPOSE

The purpose of the interview is two-fold: to learn more about your field or organization of interest and to gain additional contacts. (You will learn more about this as a vital aspect of networking in CHAPTER 3.) Each informational interview you conduct expands your network as you receive additional, relevant contacts and continue scheduling subsequent interviews. Through this process, you will likely clarify favorable and unfavorable aspects of the career you are considering, and discover related careers you had not previously considered. Quite often you will be referred to actual employment opportunities (though that is not the explicit intention of informational interviewing). As you gather new information, take time to reflect on how that career does or does not align with who you are. Are there aspects of the work environment that may or may not fit with your personality? Will you be able to use your preferred skills and have the opportunity to develop new skills? Will your values be satisfied or compromised? Your career development is a life-long process and requires continuous, conscious reflection as you learn and experience new things.

SAMPLE QUESTIONS FOR INFORMATIONAL INTERVIEWING

OCCUPATIONAL REQUIREMENTS AND EXPERIENCE

- How did you get started in this field? Is that typical of most people?

- Describe a typical week. Would these duties be the same for anyone with your job title?

- What skills and personal qualities are most important for success in this job?

OCCUPATIONAL ENVIRONMENT

- How would you describe the professional climate in your office? In your industry?

- What portions of your job involve interaction with coworkers, clients, or vendors?

- How much evening, weekend, or overtime work is required? What about traveling?

BENEFITS AND CHALLENGES

- What are the greatest rewards of your work?

- What are the greatest frustrations? How do you deal with them?

- On what basis are professionals in your field evaluated? How is success measured?

- What is the starting salary range for new professionals in this field? (Do not ask for the person's salary.)

OCCUPATIONAL OUTLOOK

- What are the opportunities for advancement in this field? Could you describe a typical promotion path?

- What are some growth areas in this field and what impact is that likely to have on job opportunities?

- How is this field likely to be affected by changes in technology?

  (continued)

21

SAMPLE QUESTIONS *(continued)*

ADVICE

- What kinds of education or specialized training would best prepare me to do this kind of work?

- What classes can I take, or what projects can I complete, that will also be helpful?

- Are there any professional organizations that would help me to build my network in this field?

- How do people find out about job openings in your line of work?

- Where do people in this field typically look for internship and job opportunities?

- Who makes the decision to hire someone for this kind of job?

HOW TO ARRANGE AN INFORMATIONAL INTERVIEW: THE PROCESS

To find someone to interview, ask friends, relatives, and others for suggestions. You can also contact faculty members, academic advisors, or your school's career center. See your school's alumni office for names and contact information of former students who are working in career fields of interest to you.

To arrange an informational interview, begin with an email request for a phone or in-person appointment. In your message, introduce yourself and explain how you received the person's contact information, what you hope to gain from the interview, and the tangible steps for scheduling the appointment.

To maximize the potential of conducting an effective informational interview, prepare your questions in advance and dress professionally. During the interview, express your appreciation of the person's time and expertise, be cognizant of their time restraints, and above all, *do not* ask for a job or internship. Ask if he or she can recommend other people you could contact to continue the exploration process. If you have additional time and sense the interviewee would be receptive to helping further, present your resume for brief, high-level feedback. The perspective of a professional who is *currently* working in your field of interest may prove

REQUESTING AN INFORMATIONAL INTERVIEW:
SAMPLE MESSAGE

Dear Max,

I am a senior at Indiana University majoring in psychology. I had the pleasure of being introduced to you through my sister last month at a holiday party, and I would like to take this opportunity to follow up with you. I am currently exploring careers in training and development. The expertise you have gained through 15 years of experience in the field would be very helpful as I continue to learn and explore this area of human resources.

Might you be available for a brief phone or in-person meeting to discuss this further? Thank you for your consideration, and I look forward to hearing from you.

Sincerely,

Sally Detwiller

to be especially beneficial as you continue to refine your resume. Following the interview, send a thank-you note and specify items from your discussion that were particularly helpful.

RESEARCHING JOB TRENDS IN YOUR CAREER FIELD

As part of your career research, make sure to investigate the latest job trends in your career field. Do projections indicate an increase or decline in the number of jobs? How is your career field affected by economic conditions, international competition, and changes in technology? All of these factors can affect your decision to enter or not enter a particular career field.

You can use a variety of resources to research your career field or industry. Some of these resources include:

- **Newspapers and Magazines.** These publications provide the latest information concerning the job outlook, and how technology and international competition are affecting a specific career field. These publications can be national, regional, or local, and often feature articles about new and emerging jobs and careers; for example, the growth of jobs in the alternative energy sector, including wind and solar energy.

- **Trade Magazines and Professional Journals.** These publications are produced by professional associations and usually include information concerning current trends and projections for a specific career field.

- *Occupational Outlook Handbook.* This publication (referred to earlier) and its website also have excellent up-to-date information regarding the newest job growth predictions and details concerning the future job outlook for many career fields.

You can ask the staff at your school's career center or ask the reference librarian for the print or online versions of these resources.

RESOURCES FOR CONDUCTING EFFECTIVE EMPLOYER RESEARCH

It is very important to research potential employers. This type of research will help you match yourself to the employer's job description when you write your cover letter and resume. You will also have more effective job interviews; the more research you do, the better prepared you will be to illustrate how you match what the employer is seeking.

For both corporate employers and privately owned businesses, you should read and study the website of the organization that you are interested in. Call the organization's human resources or public relations department to ask them to send you an annual report and brochures. The annual report, brochures, and website will give you an overview of the services and new products offered by the organization. It will also give you an idea of the organization's personality and culture to see if it would be a good "fit" for you.

- **Corporate Employers.** In order to research corporate employers you can review websites developed by Hoover's, WetFeet, and Vault. These publishers have developed both print and online resources that will help you research many corporations.

- **Privately Owned Businesses.** Private companies, unlike publicly owned ones, are not required to file open public reports about their activities, so you need to be very resourceful in order to find information about them. In addition to reviewing the organization's website and requesting written materials, you should also research newspaper and magazine articles concerning the organization.

- **International Employers.** Online directories that can help you with your search include *Directory of Foreign Firms Operating in the United States*, and *Directory of American Firms Operating in Foreign Countries*. These directories contain contact information for each organization, including mailing address, website, phone number, and email address.

- **Local or Regional Employers.** In addition to researching the company's website, it is important to check with the local Chamber of Commerce or United Way agency. These organizations may have information about local employers. Contact your local library for assistance in finding news articles concerning the company or organization.

- **Government Employers.** For the federal government, research specific federal agency websites. Review the website of interest to you and apply online for specific jobs. You can also contact by phone the college relations representative in the federal agency's human resource department to ask about hiring procedures or request additional information such as brochures and position descriptions. Remember that often the best source of information on government agencies and departments is your own informational interviewing.

Check with your school's career center or library concerning the availability of print and online resources that are cited in this section.

GETTING EXPERIENCE: TRY OUT THE CAREER

After you have researched the career field, the industry, and specific employers, try out the career or job. You can do this in a variety of ways. One way is to complete an internship where you will gain career-related experience in a career field of interest to you. An internship can help you develop skills and experience for a future job, and it can also be a source to find out about job leads. In addition, students who have had an internship are often hired for full-time positions by the same employer.

When researching a possible internship, be sure to consider these factors:

- The length of the internship and the time of year of the internship. You can have an internship in the fall, spring, or summer semesters.

- Internships may be paid or unpaid.

- You can earn academic credit for some internships, but not all of them.

Visit your school's career center for details on researching internship sites and for information on how to apply for an internship.

OTHER WAYS TO TRY OUT A CAREER:

- If you are not able to spend months at an internship, an alternative could be a job shadowing experience where you spend part of a day or an entire day observing someone doing a job of interest to you. For example, if you are interested in being a physical therapist, you could spend half a day with a physical therapist at a hospital or a sports clinic to see if you would like the job and the work environment.

- Another way to try out a career is through an externship. An externship is similar to an internship, but usually lasts only 3 to 5 days. An externship may involve completing specific job-related tasks as well as observing a professional at work. This opportunity would also allow you to have informational interviews with professionals at the work site. An externship can be a combination of experiences including an internship, job shadowing, and informational interviewing.

- Career-related volunteering experiences are a great way to try out a career. For example, if you are interested in being a curator, you can contact a museum, and see if you can volunteer in a variety of roles at the museum. Or, if you are interested in working in a human service nonprofit organization, you can contact your community's volunteer network and local United Way agency to learn about volunteer opportunities.

- Another method of getting experience is a career-related summer job. Many career fields, including computer technology and business, offer summer jobs that provide career-related experience.

- Working at an on-campus or off-campus part-time job is also an option. This experience will help you develop skills and personal qualities valuable to employers including time management, adaptability, and flexibility. In addition, you will learn to work as a team member in a professional environment. Check with your career center to learn about part-time job opportunities on your campus.

- In order to develop your skills and obtain career-related experience, become a member of a student organization on your campus. Contact your student activities office to learn about how you can become a member of a student organization. Taking a leadership role in a career-related student organization will provide you the opportunity to visit and learn about a variety of businesses. Some student organizations take field trips to various businesses and organizations, which are great opportunities to observe a business in action and to ask many questions about a specific career field.

- Many universities offer service learning courses that combine theory from an academic perspective with practice from real-life experience. These courses will connect your class work with a project in a community business or nonprofit organization. You will be providing a service and learning at the same time.

JASON'S INTERNSHIP EXPERIENCE

Jason was an economics major who decided that he needed a summer internship because everyone else he knew in his department was getting one. Unclear about his motivation, Jason didn't bother to think about what was important to him or what he was interested in learning about, nor did he take time to research potential internship opportunities in depth. Jason soon found an internship as a buyer in a major department store. But his dream of a perfect internship turned into a nightmare within weeks. Jason detested the daily activities required by the internship, and the retail environment itself. However, it was too late—he had taken the internship and committed to staying until the end. The weeks went on and by August, all he could bring himself to tell his friends was that it was the worst summer he'd ever had.

Jason realized that he could have saved himself a lot of pain and trouble by exploring and researching internship opportunities before he applied. But all was not lost. After reflecting with his career advisor, Jason realized that he had gained valuable skills and experience at the internship that he could include on his resume, including writing, organizational, and computer skills. And he had also learned a valuable lesson—that his personality and values were not a match for a career as a buyer, or even for the retail field in general. Jason crossed this career field off his list, and swore that he would take the time to explore himself and research future internships and jobs before leaping into them.

CAREER DECISION MAKING

Now that you have completed your career research, you are ready to make some career decisions. Every person likes to make career decisions in a different way. Some prefer a structured and logical approach to decision making, while others are more flexible and intuitive. A strategy that can be helpful to all people is to first reflect on your values, skills, interests, and personality. As you research career fields and specific job descriptions, keep referring back to these attributes. Keep asking yourself, is this job or career a good match for me? Remember there is rarely a perfect match.

When you read a job description, there are many questions you can ask yourself. For example:

- Does the job allow me to work in teams or independently?

- Would I enjoy the work environment?

- Will I enjoy using the skills described in the job description?

- Does the position allow me to travel as much as I like?

- What is the current and future salary potential for the job?

- Will the salary meet my lifestyle needs?

- What is the mission or purpose of my potential employer?

- Does the mission match my values?

- Would I enjoy the training and preparation needed for the job?

- What is the geographic location of the job?

- Do I want to live in an urban, suburban, small town, or rural location?

As you ask yourself these questions, it is helpful to organize your answers into a "pro and con" list for each job that you research. Ask yourself what specific aspects of the job you like (the pros), and what specific aspects of the job you don't like (the cons). The act of writing down your likes and dislikes will help you clarify your thinking and make it easier for you to make a decision. The more the job description matches who you are, the more passionate you will be about the job. And when people say they are passionate about their job, they are really saying that they have found a job that matches their values, interests, skills, and personality.

REDUCE YOUR FEAR IN MAKING A CAREER DECISION

In order to reduce your fear, think of career decision making not as one big decision, but as a series of small decisions such as: what internship to take, what career-related volunteer opportunity to take, which opportunity best matches my values, interests, skills, and personality.

Remember that you are not making a career decision for life. You can always research new careers, and you can always change your mind. It is normal to be concerned about what your parents, family, and friends think. Remember they will not be going to the job with you. You have to decide which job is the best fit for you. By researching careers, you can overcome the fear of the unknown, and you will have a better idea of how realistic your job objectives are. Because you have completed research on yourself in the previous chapter and now have researched careers, you can be confident and well informed about your career decisions.

CONCLUSION

In this chapter, you have learned how to find resources for researching careers, the importance of getting career experience, and some strategies for making career decisions. You have seen the importance of researching your career field, job descriptions, and your potential employer. This type of research is important so that you can determine if you are a good fit for a specific job or career field. This research will also help you find more job leads and assist you with matching yourself to the job description when it is time to write your cover letter and resume as well as when you participate in your job interview.

CHAPTER SUMMARY AND KEY POINTS

- Successful career development requires you to research career fields, job leads, job descriptions, and specific employers.

- There are a variety of print and online resources that can help you research careers and possible job leads.

- Trying out a career is very important to your understanding of a career and can produce job leads.

- The process for making career decisions varies by personality; however, there are many factors and strategies that can be used that are helpful to all personality types.

CHAPTER THREE

FINDING A JOB OR INTERNSHIP

"If opportunity doesn't knock, build a door."

– Milton Berle

INTRODUCTION

Understanding yourself and your career options will help you lay the groundwork for the next step in your career planning process. Being equipped with the knowledge of what you like, what is important to you, what your preferred work style is, and what you do well, and developing an awareness of potential careers is the best way to start your job search process as a well-informed job seeker. In the process of job searching, opportunities rarely fall in your lap; thus as Berle suggests, a proactive approach is necessary to "build your door." This chapter discusses the importance of considering your mindset at the outset of your job search; provides you with practical tools for finding jobs; and demonstrates the need for organization and an action-oriented approach in your job search.

LEARNING OBJECTIVES

- Understand the impact of mindset before beginning the job search process

- Learn proactive job search strategies to access the visible and invisible job markets

- Discover the need for organization and taking action

MENTAL PREPARATION

The task of finding a job can feel daunting in the beginning stages. Personal obstacles to starting your career planning may include: avoidance because of fear and sadness about leaving your current role as a student; lack of direction in where to begin the search process; lack of knowledge and tools for conducting an effective search; fear of the unknown; lack of confidence in one's self, education, or experience; lack of motivation; external pressure from family, friends, and faculty. You can overcome each of these challenges by gaining knowledge and experience through careful planning. Before beginning the active steps of the search process, pause to inventory your current attitude. Determine whether or not you have limiting beliefs regarding your job search. Process each of these items individually or with the help of a trusted friend or professional. When you acknowledge your current mental outlook, you will be empowered to choose your frame of mind.

Generally, the focus of your attention becomes your reality. Deciding to believe that real and exciting employment opportunities are possible and within your reach can boost the effort and energy you invest in your job search. Allow yourself to consider your career aspirations and dreams freely. Consider the knowledge you have gained about yourself and the world of work. Set your intentions and trust that through honoring your passions and fully engaging in the job search process, your path will become open and clear. Remember, you are choosing the *next best step* in your career; you are *not* making a life-long commitment.

THE "INVISIBLE" JOB MARKET

A critical concept of job searching is knowledge of the "invisible" job market, also known as the "hidden" job market. The term refers to positions that are not posted to the public. For example, perhaps a colleague is transferring to another location in the near future, resulting in an upcoming opening in that office. Anyone outside of the organization would not know about the position that is soon to be open, making it "invisible" to the rest of the world. According to the Bureau of Labor Statistics, over half of positions are never advertised and employers fill the majority of their positions through the invisible job market. Given these facts, it is critical that you spend the bulk of your job searching time pursuing *this* job market.

So how can you discover these openings if they are "invisible?" The primary way is through information gained from other people; therefore, relationships are the cornerstone of an effective job search. It is natural to direct your attention to the Internet when strategizing ways to find current employment opportunities. Online job boards, company websites, and interactive recruitment systems are useful for locating potential jobs, but they should not be the only tools you use. Though technology has dramatically increased the dissemination of information and the efficiency in collecting candidate application materials, the use of personal connections and networking continues to be the most successful job search strategy.

What enters your mind when you hear the word networking? Do you feel excited to connect with new people? Do you picture large-scale networking events and feel anxious at the thought of facing a room full of people you don't know? Do you fear being perceived as "insincere" by others? Do you wonder what networking really means? As noted in CHAPTER 1, it is helpful to explore and understand your beliefs about yourself and the job search process. There are many thoughts and feelings associated with the concept of networking and it is essential to explore your perceptions, which may either help or detract from your ability to successfully use networking as a job searching tool.

Before discussing strategies for using and increasing your network, review what you have learned in CHAPTER 2 about informational interviewing. Networking is defined as the exchange of information, contacts, or resources between two or more people for a mutually beneficial purpose; thus, informational interviewing is one of the most effective resources for expanding your network. This kind of exchange does not necessarily have to be career related. For example, if you move to a new city and are searching for a reliable mechanic, asking your neighbors or coworkers for a referral would be a form of networking. In the context of the job search, networking is sharing information and contacts related to careers.

NETWORKING AS JOB SEARCH SKILL

So why is networking the most effective job search strategy? Put yourself in the shoes of an employer who is hiring candidates to fill positions. Would you prefer to interview a candidate referred to you by a colleague, friend, or acquaintance, or would you rather sift through dozens or hundreds of resumes from people you know nothing about, except for the contents of a resume and cover letter? Might you take more time to consider a candidate you met at a career fair, networking event, professional association, or an informational meeting? Having a relational connection will likely set you apart from your competition.

Many students fear that people will not want to help. Remember that networking is a two-way relationship designed to be mutually advantageous. Think about what you might be able to offer to a contact at this point in your career. What significant information do you have? What relevant contacts might you be able to share? You might have more to offer than you realize, and certainly in the future you will continue to gain valuable relationships and expertise to offer back. In addition to the value you bring to the relationship, consider the fact that every person has been in your shoes at some point in their life. People can empathize with the challenges of initially entering the workforce, and often find satisfaction helping others navigate their way through this unknown territory.

GETTING STARTED

The first step in this process is activating your current network. Who are all the people you currently know? You are connected to friends, family members, teachers, faculty, coaches, doctors, coworkers, past and present supervisors, academic and career advisors, and many others. Begin by reconnecting with your network to update them on the latest events of your life as well as your plans for the future. One simple and time efficient way to do this is by crafting a general email message to send out en masse or to customize to individual recipients. Activities 3.1 and 3.2 in the APPENDIX will assist you in developing your list of current contacts and writing an initial email or letter.

EXPANDING YOUR NETWORK

Prepared with the tools to activate your current network and conduct informational interviews, you are ready to learn other methods of expanding your network. One of the most obvious and accessible resources to utilize in making connections with potential employers is your school's career office. You may have access to on-campus interviews, employer information sessions, specialized career programs, networking events, and career fairs. These services and events offer you direct contact with employers who are specifically targeting students from your school. Visit your career office right away, as recruitment activities usually begin early in the fall semester.

A resource that is widely underutilized in the career search process is your alumni network. The shared experience of attending the same university as an undergraduate or graduate student provides an immediate commonality for building a connection. Most alumni associations have an online directory that allows you to search alumni contacts by city, state, major, job title, and organization. This is an excellent way to reach out to alumni who will likely have knowledge and experience directly related to your distinct interests. Depending on the size of your institution, there may be established alumni chapters both nationally and internationally. Researching those chapter contacts and scheduled events provides another avenue for connecting with alumni.

Joining professional associations is another strategic method for increasing your network. Professional associations govern the behavior and ethical guidelines of a given field and exist primarily to provide training and professional development to their members. They often offer current and relevant resources, including networking events, professional conferences, training, certifications, lectures, online resources, and job postings for openings in their field. Researching professional associations related to your career interests and joining one or multiple organizations is an effective way to facilitate your career exploration and expand your network. Most associations offer a reduced rate for students or new professionals and some have campus chapters. Including these memberships on your resume demonstrates to employers the commitment you have made to that field.

WHY NETWORKING?

While it is so tempting to ignore the great emphasis being placed on networking in this chapter, resist taking the path of least resistance. Even though online postings do exist, the fact that only 20–50% of open positions are ever publically advertised means that you will miss out on many opportunities if you do not take the time to gather information and establish or rekindle relationships through networking. Begin with the relationships you already have. Remember your network is not just the group of people you actually know, but it also includes everyone they know. Put your network to work for you, and remember to look for ways to give back along the way.

Attending events sponsored by your local Chamber of Commerce is another powerful resource for making additional contacts. Chamber of Commerce organizations exist in almost every city and town to promote the local businesses in their community. Most chambers hold regular professional and social networking events which many local and regional organizations attend to exchange ideas, information, and contacts. The Chamber of Commerce may also offer suggestions and contact information for other local networking groups such as the Rainmakers, Young Professionals, and Business Networking International (BNI). If you feel intimidated attending such functions alone, consider going with a friend who is also conducting a job search.

Utilizing online networks is also a useful tool in gaining new contacts or reconnecting with people with whom you have lost touch. Social networking sites are primarily geared toward personal rather than professional connections, though you can use social contacts to expand your network. On the other hand, professional networking sites are designed to connect people in the context of careers. These online tools are similar to social networks, but are a more cautious choice because they do not contain personal information and tend to focus on work-related topics. Whether you are using social or professional online tools, consider the general guidelines listed below.

Do's of online networking:

- Notify your current contacts of your upcoming job search
- Join relevant groups (alumni; previous, current, or potential employers)
- Request introductions to your contacts' connections
- Search for jobs
- Create and use an appropriate email address
- Utilize your privacy settings (for social networks)
- Google yourself to ensure you have a "professional" online presence

Don'ts of online networking:

- Accept people in your network who are strangers or with whom you have no connection
- Broadcast your membership in potentially controversial online groups
- Publicize your phone number or home address
- Post unprofessional status changes

GETTING YOUR FOOT IN THE DOOR: ACCESSING THE INVISIBLE JOB MARKET

As a new professional seeking to launch your career, keep an open mind and be creative as you strategize how to land your first full-time job. While some organizations will have entry-level positions intended for recent college graduates, many worthwhile organizations will not have such overt points of access. This section provides alternative methods for entering fields and organizations of interest to you. These techniques are not suggested as permanent solutions, but rather as a means for entering organizations or fields in which full-time employment is not readily available.

- **Volunteering.** Becoming a volunteer is an excellent way to gain needed experience, build contacts within an organization and occupational field, and demonstrate your talent to a potential employer. You may need to consider working a part-time job to cover financial expenses during your time serving as a volunteer.

- **Part-time jobs.** Getting a part-time job is another entry point into an organization. Budgets may not permit full-time positions at the time of your job search; however, through taking a part-time position, you are proving your value to your employer and building relationships that may translate into a full-time opportunity in the near future.

- **Post-graduate internships.** Some employers offer post-graduate internships. This is a win-win strategy for you to "test drive" a job and an organization to determine your interest and fit, and for the employer to assess your skills, work ethic, and organizational fit. Taking an internship after graduating can be a valuable next step.

- **Employment firms and temporary employment agencies.** Private employment firms, also known as staffing agencies, are organizations hired by employers to find talent in an effort to meet staffing needs. Be aware that employment agencies are seeking to meet the needs of their clients and may not prioritize your career interests. It is your responsibility to critically evaluate the fit of both the job itself and the work environment. You should not be required to pay a fee for these services because most employment agencies are paid by their clients to find talent. Be cautious about working with agencies that charge you a fee for services.

- **State and federal unemployment agencies.** These agencies, funded by the government, provide skill assessments as well as professional training to increase your employability. You can find information about local agencies through your career center website or campus library.

THE "VISIBLE" JOB MARKET

Up to this point, we have discussed job and internship search strategies that target the "invisible" job market and require you to be proactive in making connections with people, organizations, and opportunities. You will now learn how to enter the "visible" job market (positions that are publicly posted), a resource that allows you to be more passive as you simultaneously pursue your job search using the methods previously discussed. In this section, we will review resources to help you find advertised job openings and discover potential employers. Resources you can use include:

- **Online Job Boards.** Take advantage of the online recruitment software provided by your career services office by creating a profile, uploading your resume, and applying to internship and job postings. Additionally, your career center may have purchased online job and internship subscriptions (visit your career center's website) that provide employment opportunities in specific career areas such as sports, entertainment, the arts, and nonprofit organizations. You can also create profiles and upload resumes on large job boards. Typically you can initiate a job agent, defined by your unique interests, which will email you periodically with new postings. Use caution as you interact with job boards; if you are unfamiliar with an organization, conduct extensive research to verify the validity of the organization. Be aware of employers that require you to purchase products or services upfront. Additionally, when conducting your search, resist the urge to use *only* online resources; though it may feel more comfortable, require less time, and produce immediate results initially, it lacks the comprehensiveness needed to achieve a successful job search, plus you are competing with the other hundreds or thousands of job seekers who have also applied.

- **Employer Directories.** Although the directories will not list current job openings, they can help you find potential employers in a specific career field or geographic area. You can send your resume, send an email, or make a phone call to these employers. The directories include contact information, email address, website, mailing address, and phone number. For example, the *Sports Market Place Directory* is an employer directory for students interested in a job or an internship in the sports field. You may find these resources in your career, campus, or public library.

- **Trade Magazines and Professional Journals**. Many trade magazines and professional journals include job listings or contact information of potential employers. For example, *Biotech Business* is one of the trade journals for the biotechnology industry.

- **Chamber of Commerce Directories.** Chamber of Commerce organizations usually have printed and online directories that provide contact information for specific businesses and nonprofit organizations. Once you have identified organizations of interest, go to the careers portion of their website and complete an online application or upload your resume. Again, you will be notified when a position for which you are qualified becomes available.

- **United Way Directories.** If you are interested in social service or non-profit job opportunities, one resource is the United Way chapter in your local community. Most United Way chapters publish a membership directory that gives contact information that can be very helpful for your job search.

LUCY'S JOB SEARCH PLIGHT

Lucy was a senior majoring in communication. It was holiday break and she was at home being asked repeatedly by her parents about her post-graduation plans. Believing it was most important for her to focus solely on her studies, she was unwilling to launch her job search five months before graduation. After all, wasn't there still plenty of time? To get her parents off her back, she agreed to speak with a friend of the family who was a career counselor, who provided many ideas and suggestions for executing a successful job search—including the importance of starting now. But instead, Lucy returned to school for the spring semester and continued to avoid the job search.

With graduation nearing and many of her friends excitedly sharing good news of their job offers and acceptances, Lucy began to wonder if perhaps she should be starting this whole "job search thing." She felt frightened. "What do I want to do? Will anyone want to hire me? What if I get stuck in a job I hate?" Paralyzed by her fear, she put off the search until after graduation.

After graduating, she decided to post her resume on all the big job boards. She checked her email every day and wondered why her inbox was not full of employment opportunities waiting just for her. At this point she frantically started asking her family for help. Did anyone know about any job openings? Her brother provided an introduction to a social service agency for which he worked. Lucy hurriedly asked for a crash course from her career counselor, and had an interview with her brother's employer the next week. Lucy received an offer and accepted immediately. She began her new job and soon realized she was uncomfortable with her work environment, she couldn't stand her boss, and she did not enjoy the work itself. "Now what?" she wondered, trying to calm the panic welling up inside. She decided to try as hard as she could and make it work, no matter what. After three months of misery and daily questioning of her next step, she turned in a two-week notice.

She spent the next two months wondering what had happened. She felt like a failure. She was unsure of the future. Finally, one day she realized that she needed to take time to reflect on what she had learned and to consider the advice she had been given. She realized how much time and energy she would need to dedicate to this process. She realized all the opportunities she had missed to connect with employers and professionals through her university. She realized how many organizations had already filled their entry-level positions. She chose that day to start over, get organized, take action, and launch an intentional, well-balanced job search.

THE BIG PICTURE: CRAFTING YOUR JOB SEARCH ACTION PLAN

As you can see, searching for a job is at least a part-time, if not a full-time, job. You must systematically dedicate time to the search to be able to execute a balanced job search and employ as many of the strategies discussed as possible. According to data from the Bureau of Labor Statistics, job seekers who use many search tactics are more successful than those who use one or two. As mentioned before, the bulk of your job search should be spent engaging the invisible job market through networking, and a small portion should be spent locating the visible job market via online resources. If you are feeling stuck, step back and evaluate which strategies you are using and how you are implementing them. Perhaps you need to shift your focus or expand your efforts. It is essential that you develop an organized system to track all the activity associated with your job search, including your growing network, positions for which you have applied, events you have attended, and organizations you are pursuing. Be intentional about nurturing your network throughout your search process, and even after you begin your career. Activity 3.3 in the APPENDIX will help you organize both your contacts and your job searching strategies.

CONCLUSION

You have learned about choosing your mindset and being proactive in the job search process. Remember to employ a balanced search with a primary focus on networking. Despite your newfound awareness and your evolving job searching skills, expect to encounter challenges, disappointments, and frustrations along the way. Expanding your network may be awkward at first. Interviewing may be clumsy. Organizations may reject you based on your lack of skills or fit within their environment. It is all part of the job searching experience. It is most important that you evaluate each encounter and notice what you are learning about yourself (skills, values, interests, personality, and beliefs) as well as the world of work. Trust the process and take time to reflect and to congratulate yourself on your efforts and successes. Find a trusted mentor or professional to help you gain momentum when you feel down, provide pointers on your strengths and weaknesses, and help guide your decision making. Like any plunge into the unknown, the job search can be exciting, distressing, and ultimately fulfilling. Whatever barriers you may encounter along the way, if you maintain a positive outlook, you're sure to find the way to your destination, and to look back with satisfaction on your journey.

START NOW!

Though you may be inclined to delay getting started on your job search process, it is critical that you begin now! It is natural to feel fear or sadness in moving on to the next stage of your life, but the sooner you get active in the process, the more confident you will become and the more opportunities you will have. Another reason to start now: You have many valuable resources at your fingertips while you are *still on campus*. Start small—take one action in the next 24 hours to advance your job search, and continue your process one day at a time.

CHAPTER SUMMARY AND KEY POINTS

- Awareness of your mindset, your attitude, and intentions greatly affects the job search process.

- Your job search should focus on proactive strategies to build your network and access the invisible job market.

- Success depends on organizing your job search, developing an action plan, and staying dedicated to a consistent search.

RESUMES

"If you're trying to persuade people to do something, or buy something…you should use their language, the language in which they think." – David Ogilvy

INTRODUCTION

Prospective employers often know you only as a resume and a cover letter. These documents must argue for you in your absence and, somehow, convince their reader that you can do a particular job very well. This single task is hard enough, but to make it even worse, you will be lucky if an employer spends more than 15–20 seconds reading your resume, and your competition can be vast. This chapter and the next will teach you—as Ogilvy suggests in the quote above— to use the employer's words to make your job application persuasive, giving you a way of understanding resumes and cover letters that you can use throughout your life.

LEARNING OBJECTIVES

- Understand the purpose of a resume and how it can be used as a customized personal marketing tool

- Be able to apply the standards of professional language and communication and traditional resume formats

- Know how to write accomplishment statements that clearly and compellingly promote your strengths and skills

THE PERSUASIVE RESUME

When writing any document, you must keep in mind the situation: To whom are you writing? Why are you writing? What words can you use to get what you want? For a student seeking a job or internship, answering these questions is easy:

- You are writing to a potential employer.
- You want this employer to hire you for a specific position.
- Your words must convince the employer that you are the best person for the position.

This seems simple, but people often misconceive the purpose of a resume. Keep in mind that a resume is simply your response to the job-hunting situation. A resume is not a complete history of your work, a whole representation of yourself and your interests, or a job application form. The purpose of the resume is to convince the reader that your past experience proves that you can do the tasks required by the present job or internship. If the resume succeeds, you will be offered an interview to prove it in person.

The most familiar analogue to a resume is probably an advertisement. If it's helpful to you, think of your resume as a marketing device with a single customer, the employer. Remember that marketing does not demand full disclosure. McDonald's doesn't include a calorie count or a history of the company in its ads to sell hamburgers. Your resume should include only the most relevant, persuasive information about yourself.

So what do employers find persuasive and relevant? The rest of the chapter will answer this at length, but the answer isn't complicated. Primarily, the employer needs to believe that you can accomplish all the individual tasks associated with the position. Beyond this, you must also prove that you are "professional," meaning that you know all the unspoken standards of language, presentation, and process. We'll go over these unspoken standards first, because they determine the formatting and general outline of your resume. You must, however, go beyond just these basics; a resume that is not customized for a particular position is less likely to persuade the reader to give you an interview.

Because your resume stands in for you until the interview, you need to understand all the elements that let you control how you are seen even when you aren't physically present:

- **The process.** To a certain extent, you choose how and when to contact your potential employer. You may be required to submit an email or letter, but you control the details of submission as well as the follow-up. You might include portfolio material, link to a website, and call or email periodically to remind the employer of your interest.

- **The format of documents.** In almost every case, you want to match the employer's expectations here. Your resume and cover letter should stand out for the qualifications they present, not because they look odd.

- **The choice of topics and content.** Although many students think their past experience is limited, in fact there is nearly always too much to choose from. Even a position as humble as a volunteer soccer coach offers many choices for a job or internship application: Would you emphasize the management or the mentoring aspect? Would you discuss your coaching methodology in depth or instead talk about where the position led you?

- **Style, word choice, and grammar.** Maybe your old bosses sucked and the job didn't do jack for you, but presenting yourself and your past in those terms won't improve things. One of the unspoken rules is to always appear businesslike, educated, and positive.

Resumes and cover letters are made and remade, over and over, and with striking transformations, from a single body of experience. Be aware of your raw material. All the coursework, volunteering, and extracurricular and paid work you have done can be selectively trimmed and shaped into a job application. Activity 4.1 in the APPENDIX will help you gather your information into one location so that it may be drawn upon when it comes time to create a customized resume.

Liberal arts students, especially, need to know how to market themselves. Your knowledge and experience are incredibly diverse and can be applied and useful to almost any field. But because most majors don't have a direct job path (such as an accounting major becoming an accountant), it is up to you to make a persuasive case for yourself. With a carefully crafted resume, a history major can make a compelling case for a position in marketing, and a psychology major could land a position in information technology.

Before we go further, though, you need to know the standards of resume-writing. Your documents should follow some basic rules, and you can even tweak these to make your resume stand out and be more persuasive.

EVAN'S RESUME

It had been almost four months since he sent out his first set of job application materials. Since then, Evan, a senior double majoring in history and English, had sent well over 60 resumes and cover letters to various employers and posted his resume on several job board websites. His frustration was mounting and was compounded by the fact that his less-experienced friends seemed to be having more success with their job searches. "How are they getting interviews and I'm not?" Evan wondered.

Evan decided to seek advice from Pam, his former supervisor and now a mentor, from the internship he had last year with a local nonprofit organization. Upon sitting down in Pam's office, Evan said "Here is the resume I've been using."

"*The* resume?" Pam asked.

Pam was taken aback slightly. Evan was a very bright young man, so she was surprised he had not made the connection that a single resume was probably not the best strategy for getting interviews. She explained that every organization is different and with hundreds of candidates to sift through, organizations are more likely to invite candidates to interview who can translate their experience into the skills and knowledge needed for the particular position. After discussing his resume further, she recommended Evan visit his school's career center to utilize their career resources for research and to get more advice about creating targeted resumes.

With his career advisor's help, Evan was able to master the art of creating targeted resumes, which he came to realize involved a lot more research than he had been doing previously. Though the application materials for each position took longer to generate and resulted in his applying for far fewer positions, he was beginning to see a return on his investment. His first seven applications resulted in four interviews. Excited about his new-found success, Evan even reapplied for some of the positions he did not receive an interview for earlier. His research, he feels, has also given him a head start with the interview process!

RESUME STANDARDS

Your potential employer has an image of the perfect candidate; the hiring process is just a matter of comparing applicants to the imagined ideal. The job announcement likely describes the duties of the position and what qualifications are sought. Do not try to surprise your potential boss by deviating from standard resume-writing procedures and mechanics. While you do want to avoid thinking of a resume as a template that your information is plugged into, by recognizing and skillfully employing the resume standards outlined in this chapter, you can effectively and immediately convey your qualifications to the reader.

These standards arise from three basic principles:

- Focus on the strongest aspects of your past experience.
- Clearly convey your skills so that the reader connects, without thinking, what you did before to what you can do in the future.
- Concisely describe what you did so the reader learns the most relevant information in the fewest words.

These three principles give you a way of judging whether a resume is good or bad: a good resume clearly and concisely shows your strongest attributes, a bad one does not. Although there are several basic outlines (which we call chronological, functional, and combination resumes), and innumerable templates and formats, they are not all equal. Pick the best for your situation.

Some general rules and common mistakes arise from these principles:

- **Exclude high school information**. Most of your competition will not include this information; if you do, you run the risk of setting yourself apart as someone too young and inexperienced for the position. Ignore this rule only if you apply to work at your high school, or in circumstances where the experience was highly relevant and you have no other such experience.

- **Exclude personal information**. This includes personal interests, age, race, religion, and a photograph. These do not convince the employer you can do the job, so they are extraneous.

- **Use every word wisely**. Include an objective statement only if it does something to convince the reader to hire you rather than your competition. Rather than inexpressive category titles like "Work Experience" or "Relevant Experience," use titles that target the job, like "Management Experience," "Sales Experience," etc. Avoid listing memberships, unless they contribute to your resume; if you were very active as a member or held leadership positions, you might consider including them as a specific experience with accomplishment statements.

- **Use plain, businesslike English**. It's easy to fall into clichéd resume-speak and throw around phrases you would never hear (like "utilized customer service skills"). Your reader doesn't talk like this either, and such language just impedes comprehension. When in doubt, use the same language you would use to explain your skills and tasks to your grandmother. Rather than "utilized customer service skills," you probably "resolved customers' complaints" or "explained the organization's policies." At the same time, avoid being too casual. Your reader is classy. You did not "receive a full ride" or "order around subordinates"—you "received full support" and "created task lists for supervised employees."

- **Use minimal style and formatting**. Try to leave white space in your resume, use no more than two font types and no more than three font sizes, avoid underlining text, and add style only when needed. Tasteful formatting and the occasional use of horizontal or vertical lines can enhance your resume. See the examples later in this chapter.

- **Within categories, use reverse chronological order.** Within each category, go from the newest experience to the oldest, by end date. To avoid putting an unimpressive, recent job at the top, break it out into another category; see Figure 1 (p. 68) for a model. Functional resumes have some freedom from this rule; see Figure 4 (p. 74).

- **Deliver your materials professionally.** Use a large envelope so you do not need to fold your materials if you mail your job application, and print your resume on high-quality resume paper. If you email your materials or a follow-up message, use business-like language, good grammar, and perfect spelling. If you phone to follow up, use "Dr.," "Mr.," or "Ms." (never "Mrs." or "Miss"), and be brief.

SHARED ELEMENTS FOR ALL RESUME FORMATS

All resumes share some basic elements that can help convince your potential employer that your past experience qualifies you for the present position.

CONTACT INFORMATION

Your employer needs to know where to contact you. A common error for students is to include two addresses with no guidance as to when to use each one. If you must include two addresses because you really don't know where you'll be, then give a date range:

(Until July 31)   (After July 31)
625 N. Jordan Ave.   625 S. State St.
Bloomington, IN 47405   Ann Arbor, MI 48109

OBJECTIVE STATEMENT

Don't let your email or cell phone make you look unprofessional! Use a professional-sounding email address, preferably either your name or some combination of your first and last name issued by your university (e.g., gsmiles@indiana.edu). Your voicemail greeting should also be professional and to the point. If you're able to set a special ring that the caller hears, disable it while you're hunting for a job or internship.

An objective statement, which is optional, automatically limits your resume. It designates an area you want to highlight, to the exclusion of other areas. Make this work for you by tailoring every objective statement to a particular type of career field and organization. Otherwise, either use it to highlight something really spectacular ("Individual with five years' experience in management") or leave it out. Always highlight what you offer to the employer, not what you want to gain:

- *Employer-focused* objective. Seeking an internship position in event planning where I can use my organizational skills and experience in graphic design.
- *Self-centered* objective. Seeking a position where I can work in graphic design or event planning to gain experience and prepare for a future career in marketing.

If you are posting your resume on a job board where you want it to be seen by a variety of potential employers, write an objective that is as specific as possible while leaving it applicable to the various fields of interest you have. If you are attending a career fair, you could take the same approach, but it would be even better to craft several different resumes geared toward the various types of employers who will be attending. (There is usually a list of employers who will be attending the career fair available prior to the event.)

EDUCATION

Because it is usually their most relevant experience, college students and recent graduates should place the education section near the top of the resume. As experience is gained, the education section is sometimes moved to a subordinate position on the resume. The education section includes the basics—graduating university name and location, expected date of graduation, type of degree, major, and minor—but can also include other learned skills. You can include lab skills, foreign language proficiencies, software skills, and certifications, if they're relevant to the position. If you do include skills, it's most convincing to put them in some sort of context: a single line, "Photoshop," is much less persuasive than "Photoshop: Created event flyers, media packaging," and so on. You may also decide to create an entire section of your resume devoted to particular skills, but you do so at the risk of not conveying to your reader where or how you gained the skills. You don't need to include any universities or colleges other than the one you're currently attending, but if for some reason they are relevant to the position, go ahead. Include your GPA only if it's over 3.0 on a 4.0 scale.

EXPERIENCE

Your work experience and skills might be divided into any combination of categories; see the examples later in this chapter. However, you will usually describe your experience in very standard, pithy, bulleted phrases. These phrases—statements of what you have accomplished—allow employers to see at a glance what you offer. Writing these phrases can be daunting, but the next section gives you a formula and some tips to follow.

FOREIGN LANGUAGE SKILL QUALIFIERS

Consider using the following words to qualify your foreign language skills:

- **Literate.** Can comfortably read and write the language.

- **Conversational.** Can speak the language.

- **Proficient.** Can read, write, and speak the language well.

- **Fluent.** Can read, write, and speak the language with similar skill to a native speaker. (You must be prepared to be interviewed and work in this language.)

LISTING EXPERIENCE WITH RELIGIOUS
OR POLITICAL ORGANIZATIONS

While the main focus of your resume will be your skills and accomplishments, the experiences you list may also imply your values and interests. This can be a sensitive situation when it comes to listing affiliations or experiences you've had with religious or political organizations.

Of course, if you are applying for a position at a religious or political organization, such experiences you've had can be highly relevant to the position and increase your chances of earning an interview. But when applying to positions that are not religiously or politically oriented, consider the following when deciding whether to include the experience:

- Are there other recent experiences that may not be as controversial where you could include an accomplishment statement that reflects the skill or knowledge you are trying to express?

- Is that skill or accomplishment necessary to express for the particular position?

- Given your perceptions about the organization and position, is there a chance the inclusion of such information will have a negative impact on your candidacy?

Ultimately, the decision is yours. Just know that there is always some risk in including personal information on a resume—and your involvement with some organizations might lead an employer to make assumptions about you because of experiences you've listed. You will need to weigh the risks against the potential benefits.

ACCOMPLISHMENT STATEMENTS

An employer should be able to glance at your resume and immediately understand which skills you bring. Begin each of your accomplishment statements with the skill you used. This parallel structure creates a basic list of skills on the left side of the page. Your reader will also be curious about the details. What was the scope of your work—big or little, broad or focused? Why did it need to be done? Did it work?

Taken all together, you must consider (but not necessarily answer) all of these questions:

- **What did you do?**
- **How did you do it?** In person, by phone, using a particular software package, etc.?
- **How much or how many?** How many things, people, or dollars were involved?
- **Why did you do it?** Why did anyone need to do it?
- **How did it end?**

Do not include all of this information all the time! Only include what's needed to convey what you did and to get the interview. Use the appropriate tense—present tense ("Serve customers") if you are still doing it, past tense ("Initiated a new server training plan") if you are not still doing it or if the action is completed.

Some examples:

- Designed 4 new activity programs to educate 75 summer campers
- Scouted locations, acquired permission to film, obtained props
- Collaborated with committee to select topics for and facilitate 12 public awareness and entertainment programs for Indiana University students
- Created and placed displays to effectively market new products and store promotions

The first example focuses on the "how much" and the "why" questions. The writer doesn't mention any particular method because that information is uninteresting and irrelevant. The second example similarly sticks to the most interesting information, in this case simply the "what" question. The third and fourth examples elaborate quite a bit more because the skills—"collaborated" and "created displays"—would be meaningless without the extra information.

The importance of action verbs is commonly stressed in resume writing. Certainly, you want to begin with a verb, because verbs more vividly persuade the reader that you can do things. However, the verb must also be meaningful and skill-based. Only you can describe what you did and why it was impressive. Start with an honest assessment: why were you an asset to the previous employer, and how will you be an asset to the next? Later in this chapter, we'll discuss how the employer's job or internship posting can guide your writing.

Finally, avoid all-purpose words that summarize a set of skills rather than listing those skills individually. If you managed a group of people, break that into the component skills: you taught, mentored, scheduled, resolved conflicts, etc. Avoid summary words like "worked," "did," and "oversaw," as well as words that convey no concrete skills, like "helped," "assisted," "learned," "mastered," "observed," "accomplished," "honored," and "achieved."

RESUME FORMATS

There are three popular resume formats: (1) the reverse-chronological resume, which emphasizes past experiences; (2) the functional resume, which emphasizes sets of skills; and (3) the combination resume, which has a section showcasing skills and a section with past experience.

REVERSE-CHRONOLOGICAL RESUME

The reverse-chronological resume, the most popular format, emphasizes past experiences. Students' and new graduates' reverse chronological resumes usually begin with contact information, optionally provide an objective statement, and then give a brief summary of education. After these preliminaries, the bulk of the resume is composed of "experience blocks," which each provide an organization name, location, dates of employment or activity, title of the position held, and a bulleted list of accomplishment statements:

Organization, City, State (Start Date-End Date)
Title of the position held

- Accomplishment
- Accomplishment
- Etc.

Experience blocks can come from any experience, not just paid work. Consider coursework (see Figure 2 on p. 70), positions of leadership, volunteering, and internships. Don't include everything you've ever done, though. Read the next section on customizing your resume, and think carefully about which experiences you should include and how you should craft your accomplishments. Every word of your resume should say to the employer, "All that I've ever done has been mere preparation for your exact, specific job."

A common problem with reverse-chronological resumes is that the most recent job (which must appear at the top of the category) may not be the most impressive. To solve this, create multiple categories. Rather than listing everything in a bland "Work Experience" category, have at least one targeted category and then one catchall category. For example, Ginny (see Figure 1 on p. 68) has split her experience into the targeted "Marketing and Event Planning Experience" category, and then put her other work into "Other Work Experience." Ginny has used the job announcement to guide her writing and, in doing so, has tried to match her skills with what the employer is seeking. She has done additional work, volunteering, and campus activities, but she's left those off her resume because they are not relevant to the position for which she is applying. She's only included what will help her get the interview. Notice also that she has freely mixed paid and unpaid work.

What about common sections like "Honors and Awards," "Volunteering," and so on? For the most part, these sections should be treated as experience blocks. These common sections were created by book-writers and software designers who wanted to make generic resumes that anyone could borrow. However, we are thinking about your resume as a persuasive document, not a template to be filled in. If you have honors or awards, were they part of larger accomplishments at an organization? If so, perhaps you should make an experience block for that organization. If they are related to your education, they would be most appropriate in that section. Volunteering is similar. If you did enough to merit talking about, then very likely you can create a somewhat more customized experience block;

e.g., "Community Outreach," "Teaching and Tutoring," "Leadership," or another word the employer is explicitly looking for. While "Membership" sections that just list organizations are sometimes seen on resumes, they are far less effective than describing accomplishments achieved as a member of each organization—just as you would with any other experience. What you did as a member of an organization is far more important than your simple affiliation with it; if nothing was achieved as a member, you should reconsider including it. For languages, technical skills, and other special qualifications, consider a combination resume; see Figures 5 (p. 76) and 6 (p. 78) for models.

see Figures 5 (p. 76) and 6 (p. 78)

FUNCTIONAL RESUME

Functional resumes emphasize particular sets of skills rather than extensive experience. In place of experience blocks, the functional resume usually opens with a summary of qualifications (including some "X years experience" statements) and then marks out areas of expertise. The education section is often relegated to the end. Work experience may be given, but is not usually presented in the same way as in reverse-chronological resumes.

Functional resumes share the same purposes as reverse-chronological and combination resumes, but they take a different approach. Some present a static set of skills with little context. It is a better practice, however, to contextualize your statements of "significant accomplishments" by naming organizations and places. In essence, you are organizing your resume by skill set or accomplishment blocks rather than by blocks of experience:

Information Technology Accomplishments:
- Designed and implemented complete computer networking infrastructure for Regional Medical Associates, a medical office with 120 staff members
- Developed "Dude Where's My Car" software as a course project; software now used by IU Parking Operations
- Designed and coded online store for growing ($500,000 revenue) local corn hole game materials producer

COMBINATION RESUME

Combination resumes include both experience blocks and a section covering sets of skills. For most students, the education section will be at the top, after the contact information and optional objective statement. A section of skills can follow the section on education. In Figure 5 (p. 76), Jenny has also included subcategories: within "lab skills," she has broken out the various techniques she can perform in microbiology, molecular biology, and chemistry. For students in professions that require specific technical skills, the combination resume format can usefully highlight those skills and also present a vivid, accomplishment-focused history of experience. This approach has the advantage of assuring the reader up front that certain minimum requirements have been met.

NONTRADITIONAL RESUMES

While most are likely to use a traditional resume format, there may be occasions that call for a nontraditional format. Below are some tips and guidelines for using nontraditional resumes.

- **Electronic resumes.** You'll likely communicate with potential employers via email. If the employer specifies how they want to receive your resume (mail, email, in a certain file format, etc.), you should do as they ask. But if you are given no specific instructions, you can email your resume as a file attachment. If you email or upload your resume and are given no instructions, be sure to use a widely-adopted file format, like Rich-Text Format (RTF) or Portable Document Format (PDF), that will not need to be converted.

- **Web resumes.** Web resumes are resumes written and formatted using HTML and exist as a webpage on a website. Follow the same principles for web resumes as for traditional resumes. The biggest advantage of a webpage is that you can link to portfolio material. You should make sure that your web resume does not link to any unprofessional materials you might have. A drawback, though, is that it is impossible to target a webpage to a specific employer. Should you decide to use a web resume, tailor it to, at the very least, a specific industry; do not rely upon any single, generic resume.

- **Scannable resumes.** If you see in the job posting that your resume will be scanned or should be scannable, this means that a computer will read your resume before any person does. In this case, be extra sure to use minimal formatting and clear fonts. Computer-scanned resumes tend to focus on keywords, often nouns and professional jargon. Different fields and industries prioritize their own keywords, and the system can be pretty complex. But how do you, as a humble applicant, learn these keywords? A great start is to read the employer's job posting and use as many key phrases contained in the ad as you can; we discuss this more in the next section. There are a number of resources online and in print that will help you understand how software scans resumes; you should consult them in case you need to create a scannable resume.

CHOOSING A RESUME FORMAT

Each resume format's strengths and weaknesses make it better or worse for different situations. Generally, reverse-chronological and combination resumes are more common, expected by employers, and suited to students just entering the professional world. If you work in a very transient field where it's not expected that you would have long experience with a particular organization, then consider the functional resume format. When in doubt, consult a career advisor.

Once you've made this preliminary choice, you must get to the real heart of the resume: the content. If your resume doesn't adhere to the traditional standards we've discussed, there's a good chance employers won't give it a serious read. But what should they read? How do you choose your words? These are the most important questions you need to answer in order to craft a persuasive resume.

CUSTOMIZING YOUR RESUME

You want your resume and cover letter to look exactly like the perfect application imagined in your employer's head. How do you get inside your employer's head? Do research of all types: read newspaper and magazine write-ups about the organization; read their press releases, mission statement, and "about us" section on their website; and conduct informational interviews. More than anything, the job or internship posting itself will help you. Employers don't want the hiring process to be a struggle. Often, they've done their best to write out exactly what the ideal candidate should be. In this section, you'll learn to take advantage of that.

HOW TO READ A JOB OR INTERNSHIP AD

Job and internship ads nearly always announce what sort of person the employer wants. Look for lists of duties, skills, qualifications, and requirements. Read closely, and underline all the attributes that make up the ideal candidate. Try to get a feel for the employer's personality and, especially, determine what tasks the employer needs someone to do. Here's an example of a basic, general business ad that has been marked up by a job-seeker:

> The new Clothes For You Assistant Manager will <u>work well in a team</u>, be <u>self-motivated</u>, <u>analyze</u> customer orders and supplier data sheets, and <u>communicate effectively</u> with clients. We pride ourselves on <u>customer service</u>! Selling to the heartland since 1850!

HOW TO REFLECT THE EMPLOYER'S MINDSET

After reading the ad carefully and underlining keywords, integrate the employer's mindset into your resume as thoroughly as possible. Borrow the employer's language whenever you can.

Following is an objective statement that responds to the example job ad:

> **Objective:** Seeking an Assistant Manager position in the apparel industry where I can use my customer service background and education in management to help boost sales and expand the client base.

This is an excellent objective statement because it is clear about the applicant's interest in the industry and, by borrowing words, echoes the employer's needs. The final phrase took a bit more work, though: "to help boost sales and expand our client base." Those words don't appear in the posting. Once you've stepped into the role of the person hiring you by reading and mimicking the ad, you need to go further and think about core organizational goals. These won't necessarily be the same as an organization's advertised goals, though for government and nonprofit groups it often is. In this case, the store's website probably declares a goal of "Making you look great," but more than anything else, the hiring manager just needs to sell clothes.

This example job ad also hints at how to write the resume's education section. Judging by the phrase, "Selling to the heartland since 1850," you can assume that, while foreign cultural proficiency and study abroad experience may help convey values and traits such as willingness to take risks, adaptability, and flexibility, you needn't spend a lot of space or time detailing those experiences in the resume. That space can be used for something more directly relevant.

Next, we can pick out some good category titles for the work experience sections. Because the employer wants an Assistant Manager, a "Management Experience" section would be most relevant. But an applicant with no management background could use other categories, too: "Customer Service Experience," "Sales Experience," and "Retail Experience" would all match the job.

Finally, the bulleted accomplishment statements should address the hirer's criteria. As an example, suppose an applicant had been a philanthropy chair in a Greek organization. In that role, the applicant worked with the philanthropic committee to plan and put on events and raise money for charity. This applicant could apply for the Clothes For You job using this experience block:

Management Experience
Delta Pi Pi Delta Pi, Bloomington, IN   January 2008 – July 2009
Philanthropy Chair

- Analyzed committee budget and customer base (students) to determine appropriate suppliers for food and entertainment

- Worked as part of a team to plan events and sell tickets for charity

- Communicated with administration to obtain permission for events and with students to get feedback

An applicant without this sort of experience could take another approach:

Customer Service Experience
Sicily Italian Restaurant   Bloomington, IN
Server   September 2008 – December 2009

- Independently opened and closed restaurant two days a week

- Collaborated as part of server team to boost overall revenue 30%

- Communicated with newly hired servers in role as trainer

- Increased sales by persuading customers to try daily specials, additional drinks, and additional side orders

Can you spot the words and skills borrowed directly from the job ad? Both of these examples address teamwork, communication, and sales. The first touches on analysis, the second on self-motivation. What else might you include, based on the ad? The employer's emphasis on "the heartland" provides an opening. An applicant who exhausted more relevant work experience might fill in the resume with a "Community Involvement" category. An applicant with very little work experience might bring in projects from bookkeeping, accounting, or other business courses to respond to the sort of tasks implied by "customer orders" and "supplier data sheets."

Because each employer has a different set of tasks and qualifications in mind for their own particular job or internship, the resume you use for a management position will not look the same as your resume for sales, retail, marketing, writing, or something else. Eventually you will likely hone a few basic resumes, one for each field you are interested in. However, you should still target one resume to one position whenever possible. Simply putting the employer's name and the title of the position in the resume's objective statement shows greater interest on your part than just submitting something generic. Customization—understanding what the employer is seeking and how your experience can be translated to what they want—is the key to persuasion. Activity 4.2 in the APPENDIX will help you to link your experiences to the employer's needs.

LEARNING MORE

What if you don't have a job or internship posting or if the posting doesn't include much information?

First, get personal. Don't be afraid to call your potential boss and ask what they're looking for. You can also ask others in the organization if they can spare 20 minutes or so to talk to you about their employer. During the interview, you can find out what the general responsibilities of the position are, what previous employees in the role have accomplished, and get a better idea about the culture of the organization. Of course, view these conversations as a sort of pre-interview; make sure you are appreciative of their time and professional in your approach.

Second, it's useful to see what other employers have looked for in similar positions. Search for your desired position's title on big online job and internship boards. Your career center can help you find the right kind of website. Read through other postings for the position. Print out a few of the most detailed, and use these to write your resume and cover letter.

It's a good idea to do both of these things, even if you do have a good job or internship posting to work from.

CONCLUSION

Your resume stands in for you and tries to convince the employer that your past experience makes you a good fit for the current position. It streamlines and re-orders your complex past and varied experience to make it seem that you've prepared for the open position your whole life. The ideal resume tells an employer not simply that you are qualified, but that you could excel at the position and are worth bringing in for an interview.

Take great care to customize your resume and even greater care proofreading it. Have a friend proof it for you as well. Embarrassing spelling or grammar errors— or worse, the inadvertent substitution of one word for another—will greatly decrease the chances for you to get an interview. Visit your school's career office to discuss which aspects of your background are most persuasive. Ask your advisor to go over the resume yet again to make sure it's flawless.

Your resume develops as your career develops. When you do get a job, keep a log of your accomplishments. Revisit and update your "everything document" regularly. And remember that, as you seek to change jobs or careers, you will need to reword each of your accomplishments to tailor it to what is being sought in the position you desire. See Activity 4.3 in the APPENDIX for an exercise to help you review your resume.

Ginny Smiles

123 S. Main St.
Bloomington, IN 47404
(Until May 1, 2010)

gsmiles@indiana.edu
812-855-4848

960 Hastings St.
Baldwin, NY 11510
(After May 1, 2010)

OBJECTIVE
Seeking a marketing internship with a public relations firm where I can use my experience in marketing and advertising to publicize and promote clients' products and services.

EDUCATION

Indiana University — Bloomington, IN
Bachelor of Arts — May 2011
Major: Psychology; Minor: Communication and Culture
Completed Liberal Arts and Management certificate program
GPA: 3.8/4.0

MARKETING AND EVENT PLANNING EXPERIENCE

Fishers Parks and Recreation Department — Fishers, IN
Recreation Intern — Summer 2009
- Programmed 9 weeks of summer day camps for 75 children ages 6-12
- Designed and implemented four new activity programs and two new special events
- Coordinated event logistics and park rentals using Rec-Trac software
- Supervised 15 counselors, organized training, coordinated activities, and facilitated weekly staff meetings
- Wrote weekly status reports to monitor and communicate effectiveness of programs and new events

Indiana University Dance Marathon — Bloomington, IN
Lead Organizer — January–May 2009
- Promoted event to campus organizations resulting in record number of volunteers
- Supervised 300 student volunteers over the course of three 8-hour shifts

Indiana University Union Board — Bloomington, IN
Vice President for Programming — September 2008–May 2009
- Led the 5-member Budgetary Affairs Committee charged with oversight of the organization's $100,000 budget
- Evaluate performance of each of the 13 programming committees and their marketing strategies to ensure consistency with the organization's mission and budget

Assistant Director of Forums — September 2007–May 2008
- Researched topics and compiled themes for 12 public awareness and entertainment programs for Indiana University students
- Publicized programs by contacting campus groups and creating flyers with Adobe Photoshop

OTHER WORK EXPERIENCE

Outdoor Grill — Bloomington, IN
Server — September 2008–Present
- Serve 7–10 tables simultaneously per shift in fast-paced environment
- Account for about $1,200 nightly in receipts, tips, and tip-out

Looking Good Fashions — Westfield, IN
Sales Associate — Summers 2007–2008
- Created and placed displays to effectively market new products and store productions
- Promoted corporate products such as the Looking Good Fashions credit card
- Collaborated with team to stock sales floor and meet sales goals

FIGURE 1: **Reverse-chronological resume example.**

GINNY'S RESUME EXAMPLE

JOB DESCRIPTION

Marketing Intern (marketing firm)

Seeking intern to write news releases, calendar listings, and media alerts; compile and maintain media lists; collect publicity clips and assess media value; research and present findings; coordinate event logistics and assist with on-site execution. Must be a junior or senior majoring in public relations or communications. Ability to write and organize, and basic knowledge of communication tools required.

THINGS TO NOTE ABOUT GINNY'S RESUME:

- Ginny uses an objective where she emphasizes competencies that will (or should) be proven through accomplishment statements on the resume.

- Ginny makes good use of quantifiers where possible. For example, "75 children," "4 activity programs," and "12 public awareness programs."

- Her format for listing experience works especially well for someone who has held multiple positions with one organization where each position had very specific accomplishments that do not overlap from position to position, like Ginny's experience with the Union Board.

- Ginny chooses a title for her first experience block, "Marketing and Event Planning Experience," which clearly demonstrates her skills directly relevant to the internship to which she is applying.

- Ginny has split her experience into two categories to move down her recent, but less relevant, Outdoor Grill work.

Spock McFaddin

2112 N. Dogwood Ave., Bloomington IN 47405 (Until May 30th)

14 E. Quantum Blvd., Los Angeles CA 90041 (After May 30th)

(323) 254-8421 • spock@spockmcfaddin.com

EDUCATION

Indiana University, Bloomington, IN   May 2010
Bachelor of Arts
Major: Telecommunications; Minor: Business

FILM AND TELEVISION EXPERIENCE

Course Projects, Indiana University Telecommunications Dept., Bloomington, IN   September 2008 – Present
Director, Producer, Actor, and Editor
- Scripted, directed, and produced 8 short films and 1 feature-length film
- Shot movies using both film (Super 8, 35 mm, 16 mm) and digital cameras
- Edited 12 short films and 1 feature-length film using iMovie, Final Cut Pro, Avid, Sorenson, and Live Type
- Acted in a main role in 4 short films and 1 feature-length film, acted in bit part or as an extra in 10 student films
- Posted short film Professors at Work to YouTube, received over 600,000 views (http://youtube.com/watch?v=fEDCbaMbxWw)

Hoosier Date?, Indiana University Student Television, Bloomington, IN   February 2009 – October 2009
Production Coordinator
- Scouted locations, acquired permission to film, and obtained props for three of the most frequently watched episodes of Hoosier Date?
- Organized catering, chauffeuring, and guest booking, ensuring the logistical success of the program
- Supervised 3 film crew members and 10 extras prior to and during filming
- Wrote and distributed 12 press releases for publication in local and statewide media outlets
- Designed and assisted building all sets used in the production
- Set up lighting and sound; digitized video footage, and aided in all aspects of final edit

LEADERSHIP EXPERIENCE

Delta Pi Pi Delta Pi, Bloomington, IN   September 2008 – May 2009
Philanthropy Chair
- Analyzed target audience (subsets of college students) and marketed accordingly
- Led philanthropy team to organize and run campuswide Big Dance On Campus series of contests and events, raising $20,000 for muscular dystrophy charities
- Wrote monthly reports to stay accountable to fraternity's national governance
- Communicated ideas and plans to school faculty and gained permission for the events
- Supervised sub-teams who organized catering, venues, musical entertainment, and who oversaw competition to narrow down 108 Big Dance contestants to 10 finalists

FIGURE 2: **Reverse-chronological resume example.**

SPOCK'S RESUME EXAMPLE

JOB DESCRIPTION

Production Intern (production company)

Meet with clients and staff to discuss project goals and needs, coordinate script writing, storyboarding, and scout locations. Perform video shoot, including camera setup/operation, audio/lighting setup. Perform paper edits, digitize video footage, perform audio editing, animation & titling, and video editing using Final Cut Pro. Experience with designing graphical user interface designs for websites and other electronic media preferred.

THINGS TO NOTE ABOUT SPOCK'S RESUME:

- Spock has chosen not to use an objective. Remember that an objective is optional.

- He has also chosen not to disclose his GPA. This is fine, but some employers will assume its absence means a low GPA and could result in Spock being disqualified from candidacy.

- Spock has lumped all of his course projects into one experience block.

- Though Spock's fraternity experience is his most recent experience, he used his categories to get the most relevant information (as indicated by the job description) toward the top of the resume. Remember that experience only need be listed in reverse-chronological order within category.

- Notice that if you were to scan the first word of each accomplishment statement, you'd have a good idea of Spock's skills, many of which are being sought by this employer. He also does a good job of explicating through his accomplishment statements the specialized knowledge (camera types, software, etc.) he has acquired.

JANE STREITFELD

3001 W. 3rd St. Apt. 15a, Bloomington, IN 47403
jstreitfe@indiana.edu • 812-333-1332

OBJECTIVE
To obtain an entry-level buying position within the apparel industry where skills in analysis and negotiation are required.

SUMMARY OF QUALIFICATIONS
- Completed two buying internships at large retail companies and one internship with a small boutique
- Served in leadership positions with multiple organizations
- Knowledge of merchandise planning and market research

EDUCATION
Indiana University, Bloomington, IN (May 2010)
Bachelor of Science
  Major: Apparel Merchandising
  Minor: Business
  GPA: 3.56/4.0

MERCHANDISE PLANNING EXPERIENCE
- Analyzed and presented customer profile, departmental, vendor, and advertising data for the previous year and integrated visual presentation information to Charming's Department Stores merchandising team
- Formulated and wrote a six-month business plan based on prior year's sales for the Women's Professional Wear department at Charming's Department Stores that was implemented for Fiscal Year 2009–2010
- Performed physical inventory counts quarterly for make-up section at Tina's Beauty Supply

BUYING EXPERIENCE
- Maintained sales and inventory records for Tina's Beauty Supply
- Wrote purchase orders and solicited product samples from vendors and manufacturers at Charming's Department Stores and Tina's Beauty Supply
- Observed negotiations between Charming's Director of Buying and vendor representatives

DESIGN AND COMMUNICATION EXPERIENCE
- Designed clothing line based on market research and worked with production team to create sample products for Product Design course
- Collaborated with employers and university faculty to plan the Fall Chicago Trip, including scheduling site visits and transportation, while chairing the Retail Studies Organization's Professional Development Committee

WORK HISTORY
- Charming 's Department Stores (New York, NY). Merchandising Intern, Summer 2009.
- Tina's Beauty Supply (Chicago, IL). Buying Intern, Summer 2008.
- Chic Apparel (Bloomington, IN). Intern, September 2007–April 2008.

ACTIVITIES
- Retail Studies Organization (Indiana University, Bloomington, IN). Chair of Professional Development Committee, (September 2009–May 2010); Member, September 2007–Present.
- Indiana University College Republicans (Bloomington, IN). Secretary, September 2008–May 2009; Member, October 2007–Present.
- Big Brothers, Big Sisters (Bloomington, IN). Big Sister, May 2008–Present.

FIGURE 3: **Functional resume example.**

JANE'S RESUME EXAMPLE

JOB DESCRIPTION

Assistant Buyer (retail organization)

Analyze business trends, source new products and vendors, and formulate business plans under guidance of head buyer. Will also develop products for exclusive merchandise. Other responsibilities include inputting purchase orders, maintaining databases and spreadsheets, and communicating with other departments. Must possess excellent oral and written communication skills, be able to negotiate and work as part of a team. Must be creative and be able to work flexible hours in order to get the job done.

THINGS TO NOTE ABOUT JANE'S RESUME:

- Jane does not have any full-time work experience; however, she has had three internships. The functional style resume allows her to match her skills to the job announcement better than she could with a chronological resume.

- She has organized her accomplishment statements by using logical headings that match the specific requirements listed in the job announcement.

- In her accomplishment statements she included the names of her employers. This is not required for a functional resume, but can be a good idea because a common complaint of the functional format is that it's difficult to determine where skills were developed or used.

- Jane chose to include political party affiliation. Remember, she is taking a risk by doing so.

Edmund Dantès

1848 Prow Rd., Bloomington, IN 47405
edantes@indiana.edu • 812-219-7000 • mypage.iu.edu/~edantes

Summary of qualifications
- Four years' experience in professional translation of written texts
- Languages: French (native, target), English (fluent, target), Turkish (source)
- Académie Française certified translator and interpreter
- Full member of the American Translator Association and its French and Turkish equivalents

Translation areas

Technical:
- Automotive, electronics and electronic games, machines and tools, mechanical engineering, petroleum engineering

Economic:
- Accounting, annual reports, banking, business management, finance, marketing, stock market analysis

Computers:
- Computer science, software localization, programming, program manuals, websites

Other areas:
- Advertising copy, educational materials, environmental pamphlets, film scripts, scholarly writing in history and literary theory, fiction, poetry

Recent freelance projects
- Baker's Medical (September–November 2009), Bloomington, IN. Translated 250 pages of medical equipment manuals, English to French.
- The Music Store (June–August 2009), Bloomington, IN. Translated multimedia marketing materials, English to French.
- Erdem Ozan (May–July 2009), Bloomington, IN. Translated 120 pages of poetry, fiction from Turkish to English.
- Jean Delmas (January–March 2009), Bloomington, IN. Translated 40-page literary theory article from French to English.

Software used
- Translation: Trados 5 Freelance, Wordfast, Transit Satellite PE, Déjà Vu
- OS: Mac OS X, Windows XP, Windows Vista, Linux
- Word processing: Word, Publisher, Quark Xpress, PageMaker, StarOffice, vi
- Graphics and web: Photoshop, Acrobat, Illustrator, Dreamweaver, Frontpage

Education

Indiana University, Bloomington, IN (May 2010)
Bachelor of Arts, Major: Comparative Literature
Honors Thesis: *Justice and Form: Crossing the Mediterranean in Prose*
Awarded full-support fellowship to study in France, 2008–2009

FIGURE 4: **Functional resume example.**

EDMUND'S RESUME EXAMPLE

JOB DESCRIPTION

Translator/Assistant Editor (instructional design firm)

Responsible for the translation of written texts, including instructional materials and manuals, multimedia and website content from English to French. Follow guidelines set forth by account executive with regards to translation and editing. Proofread materials. Minimum requirement of Bachelor's Degree in a language-related field or certificate in translation required. Must be native speaker of target language and possess ability to use common word processing software. Experience with desktop publishing software a plus.

THINGS TO NOTE ABOUT EDMUND'S RESUME:

- Like Jane's functional resume, Edmund uses a summary of qualifications. But unlike Jane's summary, he includes information that will not later be referenced in the resume, like memberships and certifications.

- As all of his translation experience is freelance, the functional resume seemed to make more sense. Instead of focusing on categories of skills, as Jane did, Edmund organizes his experience under "Translation areas" by types of documents he translated.

- The "Recent freelance projects" section provides specific translation projects on which Edmund worked.

- Edmund's education—despite the fact it shows an interest in literature, French, and the Mediterranean—is the least relevant item on his resume. Because of this, he has listed it last.

Jenny Lucent

3428 Buckminster Ct. Bloomington IN 47408

Cell: 314-159-2653 * Home: 812-161-8033 * jlucent@indiana.edu

OBJECTIVE

Seeking a biochemistry internship where I can use my two years' experience designing experiments and conducting laboratory research.

EDUCATION

Indiana University, Bloomington, IN (May 2010)
Bachelor of Science
Major: Microbiology
Minors: Chemistry
GPA: 3.4/4.0

Lab skills:
- Microbiology: Hemagglutination, mycoplasma, viral plaque, and antibody neutralization assays; gram-positive and gram-negative bacterial culture and identification; phage therapy
- Molecular biology: PCR reactions; DNA repair, cloning, and sequencing; transposition/transduction; gene fusion
- Chemistry: Recrystallization; extraction; distillation; gas chromatography; high performance liquid chromatography

RESEARCH EXPERIENCE

Indiana University Department of Biology, Bloomington, IN (September 2009–Present)
Laboratory Technician, Laurent Geistvoll Laboratory
- Analyze ecological interactions such as herbivory, seed predation, and seed dispersal in the evolutionary trajectories of new species in the sunflower genus *Helianthus*
- Measure and analyze the introgression of insect herbivore resistance traits
- Maintain a clean and orderly laboratory environment, write and file reports every two weeks in order to track each experiment's progress

Indiana University Dept. of Medicine, Division of Clinical Pharmacology, Indianapolis, IN (Summers 2008–2009)
Research Technician
- Recorded, in great detail, individualized responses to a specific drug therapy to help researchers determine efficacy of treatment
- Performed kinetic, inhibition, and correlation analyses in human liver microsomes and experiments in expressed human cytochromes P450 to identify primary and secondary metabolic routes of exemestane and the P450s, catalyzing these reactions at therapeutically relevant concentrations

U.S. Geological Survey, Indianapolis, IN (Summers 2006–2007)
Student Trainee (Hydrology)
- Collected samples from streams and rivers throughout the state of Indiana according to USGS standards
- Analyzed samples for algal biomass and chlorophyll data and recorded information into lab logs

FIGURE 5: **Combination resume example.**

JENNY'S RESUME EXAMPLE

JOB DESCRIPTION

Lab Assistant Internship (research lab)

Seeking undergraduate student who is studying in a biology or chemistry-related field and has prior lab experience. Should work well in a goal-orientated environment and must have good quantitative skills and an ability to analyze data. Must have knowledge of polymerase chain reaction (PCR) and mammalian cell culture. General computer knowledge as well as good communication and problem solving skills are required. Grade Point Average (GPA) of 3.0 or higher preferred.

THINGS TO NOTE ABOUT JENNY'S RESUME:

- Jenny is using primarily a reverse-chronological resume format.
- She does, however, borrow from the functional format by simply listing laboratory skills without superficially stating where she acquired them. Doing so allows her to highlight some skills she might not otherwise be able to include.
- The lab skills summary includes some of the specific skills sought by the employer as mentioned in the internship announcement.

Leah Sterrenburg

14 Lambkins Ave.
Bloomington, IN 47401
812-333-8033 • leaster@indiana.edu

OBJECTIVE

To obtain an internship where I can use my foreign language skills and experience in environmental studies and public interest outreach to promote agricultural and educational development.

EDUCATION

Indiana University, Bloomington, IN (May 2010)
Bachelor of Arts
Major: International Studies; Minor: Environmental Science
GPA: 3.8/4.0

Public Interest and Environmental Projects:
- Environmental Science Thesis: "Alternative Fuels and Deforestation: A Study of Unintended Consequences"
- Publication: "Venezuelan Political Roots in Today's Culture: Challenges to the Man," *Journal of New World Studies*, no. 6 (2008) 700–746.

INTERNATIONAL WORK EXPERIENCE

- Fluent in English, Spanish, and Portuguese. Moderately proficient in French and German.
- Active secret security clearance issued by the U.S. Dept. of State, 2008.
- Spent summer of 2008 in Mexico and spearheaded successful effort to establish new rural hospital near Guadalajara with funding from the U.S. government.

LEADERSHIP EXPERIENCE

Theta Zeta Delta Multicultural Sorority, Bloomington, IN (September 2007–Present)
Vice President
- Promoted female empowerment and multicultural leadership by partnering with other cultural centers on campus in high-profile lectures and other events.
- Mentored new members, provided guidance to a group that began its own nonprofit startup, Bloomington Cares.

Indiana University Residential Programs and Services, Bloomington, IN (September 2008–May 2009)
Residence Hall Floor President
- Developed and put on 10 programs a semester for over 40 residents, with topics on health and wellness, international affairs, U. S. politics, and education.
- Resolved students' concerns, acted as ombudsman for floor residents and presented issues to Residential Programs administrators.

FIGURE 6: **Combination resume example.**

LEAH'S RESUME EXAMPLE

JOB DESCRIPTION

Restoration Education Intern (South American nonprofit organization)

Help with ecological restoration and reforestation education in four regions of South America. Photograph, record, and catalogue plant species. Teach environmental education programs for schoolchildren. Develop a comprehensive species list of the existing wildlife. Ecological training or experience desired. Be able to converse and teach in Spanish. International experience strongly preferred.

THINGS TO NOTE ABOUT LEAH'S RESUME:

- Leah's objective statement uses the personal pronoun "I." Personal pronouns are allowed in the objective statement of a resume, but because they are so rare, it is best to avoid them. Notice how her objective statement speaks to international qualifications and environmental studies, both of which are being sought by this employer.

- Leah cites some of her academic work in her education section. This is recommended only when it is highly relevant to the employer. Both of her bullets here are clearly relevant to the job description.

- She also makes use of a qualifications summary ("International Work Experience") that emphasizes relevant experiences and accomplishments to entice the reader to further examine her resume. A qualifications summary should only be used when one has a lot of experience and accomplishments that might otherwise get lost on the resume or when you wish to use a combination of smaller accomplishments from various experiences to make a single compelling argument. A qualifications summary should not be used to list random facts, ideas, or skills.

CHAPTER SUMMARY AND KEY POINTS

- Your resume is a crafted, abridged version of yourself, not a complete work history. It should be thought of as a living and ever-changing document that gets you an interview, not a job.

- Every resume you produce should be customized to a type of position, if not a specific position, and should incorporate your career research and what is published in job descriptions or announcements.

- Your writing should be guided by the principles of showing only your relevant strengths and writing clearly and concisely. Try not to diverge too greatly from traditional resume formats.

- Accomplishment statements are the most important aspect of your resume. Consider the questions "what, how, why, how much," and "with what result" for each statement and begin each with a skill-based verb.

CHAPTER FIVE

COVER LETTERS AND OTHER CORRESPONDENCE

"A blank sheet of paper." – Ernest Hemingway

INTRODUCTION

This memorable quote is how the celebrated American author replied when asked about his greatest fear. When it comes to writing, most people would agree with Hemingway. Fortunately, however, writing professional correspondence—the subject of this chapter—is much more a set of learnable skills than an art form. This chapter will introduce you to these basic skills so that you can begin to write the most effective correspondence possible for your job search.

LEARNING OBJECTIVES

- Recognize the importance and purpose of professional correspondence in the job search

- Know the guidelines and formats of successful cover letters

- Understand the basics of other types of professional correspondence

- Be aware of standard protocol for emailing professional correspondence

All professional correspondence relating to a job search shares three basic goals:

- Show that you and the employer belong in the same, professional world.

- Emphasize your most employable qualities, clearly and concisely.

- Make your qualifications memorable, vivid, and positive.

In the last chapter, you read about the first two goals regarding resumes. Professional correspondence similarly demands that you follow unspoken customs, which determine your level of professionalism. Professional correspondence also has a self-promotional aspect, just like resumes. Your letters and emails should be limited only to information that puts you in the best light. As with resumes, you should use plain English and the fewest words necessary to convey your intentions.

Your correspondence lets you represent yourself with much more depth and nuance than your resume. This chapter will teach you some basic formulas. The formatting and outlines of correspondence are very predictable, which makes it relatively easy to write. But the content—the topics you choose—makes your correspondence memorable, persuasive, and individual (or forgettable, off-putting, and generic). Unlike your resume, your letters and email are personal messages. They establish a relationship between you and the reader. Take advantage of this, and write every message—including withdrawals and resignations—so that the reader will think positively of you in the future.

COVER LETTERS

A "cover letter" is a letter that accompanies or "covers" another document—for our purposes, a resume. Although actual employers may read your documents in any order, the cover letter is meant to announce who you are, what you want, and what you have to offer. You should always send a cover letter with a resume, unless the employer explicitly states otherwise.

There are two types of cover letters: letters of inquiry and letters of application. Send a letter of inquiry to ask whether a position is open. Send a letter of application in response to a specific job or internship opening. Either letter should persuade the employer that you have researched the organization, thought about what you might do for them, and concluded that your past experience has prepared you for their needs. The two letters differ very little in substance: a letter of application will name the specific job or internship title that has been advertised, whereas a letter of inquiry may or may not specify which exact job you're interested in.

GUIDELINES

Certain guidelines endure simply from general acceptance and must be followed:

- **Use a traditional letter format.** In this book, we've used block format for all our letters because it is easiest and most common. Your return address should be at the top, followed by the date, and finally the recipient's name, title, and address. Two lines below that, type the salutation ("Dear..."). At the bottom of the letter, type a closing such as "Sincerely," and several lines below that type your name. If you will be sending your resume with the letter, type the words "Enclosure" two lines below your typed name.

- **Limit your letter to one page.** If you find that you're taking more than one page, take a moment to evaluate which of your past experiences are most relevant to this position, and omit others. It may also be helpful to meet with a career advisor to discuss ways to shorten your letter.

- **Send a customized letter.** You throw out junk mail. You don't like things that pretend to be personal messages but really aren't. Employers are not impressed by a letter that could fit any organization and almost any open position. While this does not mean you need to write an entirely new letter each time, each letter you write should be unique in your own mind, meaning that you have carefully reviewed and revised any previously used material so that you are sure it is oriented as directly as possible toward that organization. Later, you'll learn how to demonstrate that you've thought about the employer's specific needs in relation to your own skills. There are rare exceptions to this rule, such as when replying to an ad that lists no organization.

- **Address a specific, real person.** Call and ask who will be reviewing your application. If you can't tell the gender of your addressee by the name, ask. Always avoid "To Whom It May Concern." In your letter salutation, write "Dear Mr." or "Dear Ms." (never Mrs. or Miss). If you absolutely cannot find a person to address the letter to, use one of the following salutations:

  > Dear Hiring Authority:
  >
  > Dear Human Resources Manager:
  >
  > Dear Recruiter:
  >
  > Dear Sir or Madam:

- **Use professional language and a positive tone.** Your wording shouldn't be stilted—"I utilized my formal education to market to our customer base"—but at the same time, you do not want to be overly casual, personal, or lengthy. Professional writing is short, to the point, and wholly positive. Only emphasize your assets as they relate to the organization's needs. Cut everything else.

- **Have others proofread your letter.** Your cover letter needs to be flawless. In addition to carefully proofreading every word of your letter, ask a friend or career advisor for help. Double-check the recipient's name and title.

WRITING YOUR COVER LETTER

Most cover letters follow a predictable pattern. The first paragraph introduces who you are and what you want, the middle paragraphs make the case that your past experience qualifies you for the position, and the last paragraph looks to the future and thanks the reader. But the way you treat this general outline makes all the difference. Merely fill in the blanks, and your letter will be forgettable. Take the time to think about your reader, though, and the employer may start wanting you on the team.

As with the resume, first you need to get into the employer's head. The goal is to match wavelengths with your reader: speak the same language, share priorities, and demonstrate interest in the organization. Try to get a feel for new projects and initiatives going on and consider how you might contribute to these. Research of all sorts will help: informational interviews, the website, press releases, and newspaper and magazine write-ups about the organization. Again, the job or internship posting will be a big help. Read it and underline skills or qualifications that you possess. Use this information about current projects and needed skills to explicitly address how you fit into the company. Let's look at this concretely by going through the body text one paragraph at a time.

The first paragraph: You can address your three basic goals for this paragraph in as few as three sentences:

- Explain who you are and why you're writing.

- Demonstrate that you know something about the company or organization.

- Tell them why you're a good match for them.

These last two things should be so specific that you could not say them about any other organization. They should make the strongest case possible that you and the job belong to each other.

Here's an example for the first paragraph:

> I am writing to apply for the position of Assistant Manager, which is posted on your website. I admire how Clothes For You has reinvented itself in the last two years as a hipper, more underground retail outlet; your viral marketing campaign was the talk of our campus. My years of experience in customer service and my coursework in management would allow me to contribute to your company's new growth.

Note that this example mentions the employer's company name, which attracts the employer's attention, and, even better, discusses a particular project (the ad campaign). This and "your company's new growth" are both specific to the organization and demonstrate your interest in the position.

The middle paragraph(s): One or more middle paragraphs should:

- Prove that your past experience qualifies you for the present job.
- Tell a story of growth or accomplishment about a single position or project.

If you write more than one middle paragraph, be sure that each one remains focused. While there are various ways to structure middle paragraphs, you may wish to follow this outline. The first sentence can call out one of the employer's needs, which should be related to the core demands of the position or to a current project. The next sentence(s) relate(s) a very brief story about a time you encountered a similar need and succeeded in filling it. The final sentence can refer back to the employer's needs and to what you can do for them in the future.

> **The job now:** The new [position title] will need [blank] in order to [blank]. **Past experience:** As the [old position title], I did very similar work. [Etc.] **The future:** This experience will allow me to [do something very specific and very relevant to this employer and this position].

> **The job now:** The new Clothes For You Assistant Manager will need strong analytical skills to make sure supply meets demand and keep the store within its budget. **Past experience:** As the Indiana University Dance Marathon lead organizer, I did very similar work. I analyzed and catered to a customer base while sticking to a $2,000 budget. Taking student input into account, I determined how we could best match students' expectations without spending too much. I chose an inexpensive but talented local band and the best caterer in town. The event was a hit, we raised $10,000 for a children's hospital, and the student newspaper praised our food and entertainment. **The future:** This experience will enable me to quickly learn what Clothes For You customers are like, work with vendors, and balance the books.

This first sentence raises one of the employer's needs; e.g., strong analytical skills to meet customer demand and make a profit. The next sentences respond to that need. They are structured as a story, which isn't possible in the resume. Presenting your qualifications in the form of a narrative makes them more believable and memorable. But you must also directly link this past experience to the employer's present need. The final sentence places the author into the position and demonstrates how her past experience has led her to a mastery of the specific skills that the position will require.

The last paragraph: The final paragraph formulaically ties up loose ends and looks to the future; it requires little or no customization:

- Mention anything that wouldn't fit in earlier (e.g., availability).

- Mention your resume.

- Provide your contact information.

- State your plan to follow up (unless the employer specifically asks you to not follow up).

- Thank the employer for reading your application.

Here is an example:

> Please refer to my attached resume for additional information. I can be reached at [email] or [phone] with any questions. I will be out of the country April 1–8, but will be checking my email. I look forward to hearing from you soon and will contact you in a week to check on the status of my application. Thank you for your time and consideration.

NO JOB DESCRIPTION?

Every cover letter should demonstrate knowledge about the recruiting organization, as well as the specific position for which you're applying. If you haven't been able to obtain a job description:

- Research the organization

- Talk to your contact at the organization (or find one)

- Look at postings for similar jobs at other organizations

- Conduct informational interviews with those doing similar work

See CHAPTER 2 for comprehensive research advice and resources.

SUMMARY

Cover letters are not as alien or strange as they may initially seem; they're simply the words you would say to the person who might hire you, and the words you would want to hear if you were the hiring authority. Address those you write to as you would in a conversation: directly and clearly. Think about their priorities. So long as you touch these rhetorical bases in a professional way—concisely, without errors, and without fluff—your cover letter will be sound, and in fact, may significantly improve the chances that your job search will be fruitful.

OTHER CORRESPONDENCE

REMINDER LETTERS

It's a good idea to promise, in your cover letter, to follow up within two weeks. A phone call is best. The more personal the relationship you can establish with the person hiring you, the better you'll stand out. But if it's not possible to reach your contact by phone, send a reminder letter. The goals of the letter:

- Express your interest in the organization and the position.
- Briefly reiterate your qualifications.
- Ask about the hiring timeline, and mention your next follow-up.

See Figure 3 on page 95 for an example.

THANK-YOU LETTERS

Send a thank-you letter after all types of interviews, including job interviews and informational interviews. Writing one will help you stand out from the crowd. Your letter may be handwritten, typed, or emailed. While many interviewers appreciate handwritten letters, sometimes the speed and convenience of an emailed thank you is best—your choice should be based on your best judgment of the industry and the employer, your interactions with them, and the timeline. In any event, write a letter soon, as waiting more than two days to send one may be construed as neglectful. Send a letter to anyone who spent a significant amount of time talking to you, even if they weren't your official interviewer. The goals of a thank-you letter are to:

- Thank whoever spoke to you.
- Mention something new you learned that has increased your interest in the organization and position.
- Briefly reiterate your qualifications; you can take this opportunity to mention anything vital you forgot to say.

See Figure 4 on page 96 for an example.

ACCEPTANCE LETTERS

Have you been offered the job or internship you want? Even if you are offered and accept the job verbally, respond immediately in writing as well.

- Thank the employer and express your excitement without sounding intimidated or embarrassingly grateful. At the sentence level, this isn't hard: write out your thanks and excitement once, without adjectives, and then move on to other things.
- Restate the details of your new employment as you understand them, including salary, hours, start date, and other relevant information.

See Figure 5 on page 97 for an example.

WITHDRAWAL LETTERS

If you accept one job or internship offer, you need to withdraw your other applications and other offers. This may feel hypocritical, since you spent so much effort making it seem that each position was the only one you wanted, but it's a common and acceptable part of the process.

- Express thanks for the employer's time and consideration.
- Withdraw your application or decline the offer; if making the decision was difficult, say so.

- State that you have decided to work elsewhere but do not give any reasons why.

- End on a positive note.

See Figure 6 on page 98 for an example.

See Figure 6 on page 98 for an example.

RESIGNATION LETTERS

When you resign from a job (or, rarely, an internship), your goal is to leave as positive an impression as you can on your former employer. Someday, you may need a recommendation or even want to return.

- Mention if you are grateful for something about your experience. If nothing immediately comes to mind, think some more, as the expression of appreciation can go a long way toward leaving a lasting, positive impression.

- Provide a general reason why you're leaving or where you're going, although you don't need to justify why you're leaving or give very much detail.

- State when your last day will be.

- End on a positive note.

See Figure 7 on page 99 for an example.

EMAILING CORRESPONDENCE

Email is an acceptable substitute for mail in most cases. (Thank-you letters are a common exception, as noted earlier.) When using email, heed these guidelines:

- **Use a precise, short subject line.** Capitalize as you would a book title:

  (Bad) Subject: job application

  (Good) Subject: Application for Assistant Manager

  (Bad) Subject: interview

  (Good) Subject: Yesterday's Interview

- **Use a professional sounding email address.** Students often retain unprofessional addresses from high school. Would you rather hire eddiethejoker@yahoo.com or edantes@indiana.edu? Ideally, your address is either your name or a combination of your first and last names at a dot-edu domain. If you don't have an email address like that, or if your school email account is expiring, create a professional address with a free email service that does not attach its name or ads to your outgoing email.

- **Use a proper salutation ("Dear Mr." or "Dear Ms.," never "Mrs." or "Miss") followed by a colon.** If your recipient has already insisted on being addressed by his or her first name, go ahead and use that.

- **Avoid formatting.** Use the Plain Text formatting option, and avoid HTML or Rich Text formatting.

- **Use businesslike language.** Capitalize properly and make sure your grammar, spelling, and punctuation are flawless. Write your email as formally as you would a letter.

- **Use your cover letter text for your email.** You should also attach the cover letter as a separate document. If you are emailing your resume to an employer, use the text of your cover letter as the email body, skipping the addresses and date, beginning with the salutation, and cutting out the extra space where you would normally sign. Attach your resume to the email, but also attach your cover letter as a separate file. Why? Because you don't know who will initially get your email. If it's an administrative assistant, that person will likely print off all your attachments and send them on to your prospective boss.

CONCLUSION

This chapter provides numerous examples and explanations of various common types of professional correspondence. Writing correspondence is easiest if you put yourself in the place of the person you're writing to and think about what you'd like to hear. Be sincere, to the point, and positive, and you'll find that these standardized messages begin to match what you would write even if you had no guidance.

When you're just beginning to write professionally, though, it can be hard to adopt business language and to proofread your own work. Ask a friend, a current or past boss, a career advisor, or a writing tutor to read over and critique your correspondence before you send it.

Finally, always keep the individual reader in mind. Generic letters cannot establish meaningful relationships. Generic cover letters, especially, invite the reader to think of you as an impersonal, unsympathetic individual, and they make it easier to discard your application. Take the time to treat every application for what it is: an introduction to a person you've never met but would like to work with in the future.

123 Main St.
Bloomington, IN 47404

March 14, 2010

Harry Brannigan, Manager
PRMA Associates
12894 N. Dakota Ave.
Chicago, IL 60608

Dear Mr. Brannigan:

I am writing to apply for the position of Marketing Intern, which I found posted on myIUcareers. I admire how PRMA Associates has reinvented itself in the last two years as a younger, more innovative firm; your viral marketing campaign was all over our campus. Because of my years of experience in event planning and my coursework in communications, I believe I could contribute significantly to the firm's new growth.

The new PRMA Associates Marketing Intern will need strong event planning skills to make sure its customers' programs effectively communicate their vision. As the Fishers Parks and Recreation Department intern, I did very similar work. By taking into account the unique needs of each age group of our summer campers, I organized nine weeks of programs which catered to the developmental objectives of our camper populations. Additionally I conducted research and compiled sample activities to facilitate the development and execution of six new events. I also provided regular program feedback to my supervisor through weekly status reports, allowing us to improve subsequent planning. This experience will enable me to quickly learn what PRMA Associates customers are like, work directly with their account managers, and ensure an increased value to the image of their organizations.

Please refer to my attached resume for additional information. I can be reached at gsmiles@indiana.edu or 812-555-4466 with any questions. I will be out of the country April 1–8, but will be checking my email. I look forward to hearing from you soon and will contact you in a week to check on the status of my application. Thank you for your time and consideration.

Sincerely,

[Ginny would sign her name here.]

Ginny Smiles

Enclosure

FIGURE 1: **Letter of application.** Ginny has researched the company's current project and customized her letter to match her skills to the employer's needs. Note that block format is left-aligned and single-spaced; paragraphs are not indented, but are separated by blank lines.

2112 N. Dogwood Ave.
Bloomington, IN 47405

October 20, 2010

Althea Stavropoulos
WTIU
1229 E. 7th St.
Bloomington, IN 47405

Dear Ms. Stavropoulos:

I am writing to inquire about the possibility of setting up an unpaid internship as a Production Assistant. I am a senior majoring in Telecommunications at Indiana University, and I've come to appreciate and enjoy your station more every year; you feature intellectual, currently relevant shows unlike any available on other channels. I'd be very excited to contribute what I've learned from coursework and substantial hands-on experience to WTIU.

An assistant at WTIU would need to be familiar with the basic demands of programming as well as live production. As Production Coordinator on *Hoosier Date?*, an IUSTV show, I handled just such a range of tasks. I began my position there by coordinating all the necessary details to run the show: acquiring and scheduling speakers, processing location and permissions paperwork, and directing audio and lighting for live production. In addition, I took the initiative to improve our administrative processes. I set up a shared calendar to log our tasks, documented our procedures, and implemented a system for archiving our shows. This broad experience will let me quickly adapt to WTIU's administration as well as fill any live production role in the upcoming film drive.

Please refer to the enclosed resume for additional information. I can be reached at 323-555-8421 or spock@spockmcfaddin.com with any questions. I look forward to hearing from you soon and will contact you in a week to follow up. Thank you for your time and consideration.

Sincerely,

[Spock would sign his name here.]

Spock McFaddin

Enclosure

FIGURE 2: **Letter of inquiry.** Although Spock has no posted position to respond to, his letter looks much like a letter of application. He draws attention to an upcoming project where he could be useful. Note that Spock does not simply restate his resume (CHAPTER 4, Figure 2), rather he uses this opportunity to expand on one of his most relevant experiences.

2112 N. Dogwood Ave.
Bloomington, IN 47405

October 28, 2010

Althea Stavropoulos
WTIU
1229 E. 7th St.
Bloomington, IN 47405

Dear Ms. Stavropoulos:

I wanted to write and again express my interest in working at WTIU as an unpaid intern. Your station especially appeals to me because of its unique programming and the range of work it would offer.

My Telecommunications studies at Indiana University have given me a great deal of hands-on experience in every role that goes into producing and telecasting. My work on *Hoosier Date?* at IUSTV has also challenged me and given me skills that I could use at WTIU, especially in your upcoming winter fund drive.

Thank you for your time and consideration. I hope to hear from you soon. I can be reached at spock@spockmcfaddin.com, or call me at 323-555-8421.

Sincerely,

[Spock would sign his name here.]

Spock McFaddin

FIGURE 3: Reminder letter.

123 Main St.
Bloomington, IN 47404

March 21, 2010

Harry Brannigan, Manager
PRMA Associates
12894 N. Dakota Ave.
Chicago, IL 60608

Dear Mr. Brannigan:

Thank you for taking the time to interview me yesterday. It was very encouraging to hear your own story of how you began working for PRMA Associates, and I'm glad to know that the company invests in its employees' professional development. I am certain it is a good company to work for, and I would love to join you.

I was also excited to hear that you are currently in the planning stages of an advertising blitz. In addition to what we discussed yesterday, I would like you to know that as Assistant Director of Forums for the Indiana University Union Board, I successfully headed a "get-out-the-students" initiative. I would be eager to share the strategies we developed for marketing to students to help PRMA Associates in its campaign.

Please contact me at gsmiles@indiana.edu or 812-555-4466 if I can answer any questions. I hope to hear from you soon.

Sincerely,

[Ginny would sign her name here.]

Ginny Smiles

FIGURE 4: Thank-you letter.

2112 N. Dogwood Ave.
Bloomington, IN 47405

November 12, 2010

Althea Stavropoulos
WTIU
1229 E. 7th St.
Bloomington, IN 47405

Dear Ms. Stavropoulos:

I am pleased to accept your offer of an internship as we discussed over the phone. Thank you for offering me this position. I understand that it is unpaid. I am excited to meet everyone and to contribute to WTIU.

I understand that my first day will be November 18, when I will meet my immediate supervisor, Traian Basescu. I'll come in for 10 hours a week, 1–3 p.m. Monday, Wednesday, and Friday, and 2–4 p.m. on Tuesday and Thursday. I understand that some extra work might be needed for the winter fundraiser after Christmas.

I look forward to the challenges of the new position and will do all I can to help out at the station. If you need anything prior to November 18, please contact me at spock@spockmcfaddin.com or 323-555-8421.

Sincerely,

[Spock would sign his name here.]

Spock McFaddin

FIGURE 5: Acceptance letter.

3001 W. 3rd St. Apt. 15a
Bloomington, IN 47403

March 25, 2010

Samak Sundaravej
Onoster Co.
2894 E. Third St.
Bloomington, IN 47401

Dear Mr. Sundaravej:

Thank you for your offer of employment at Onoster Co. I am honored by your confidence in me.

Although many aspects of the position at Onoster appealed to me, I have received and accepted another offer of employment. This was a very difficult decision to make.

I appreciate the time and effort you have devoted to my candidacy. Thank you for your consideration, and I wish you continued success in the future.

Sincerely,

[Jane would sign her name here.]

Jane Streitfeld

FIGURE 6: **Letter of withdrawal.**

1848 Prow Rd.
Bloomington, IN 47405

May 15, 2010

Tabare Vazquez, Manager
Blackbird Night Club
516 N. Redbud Way
Bloomington, IN 47404

Dear Mr. Vazquez:

I am writing to let you know that I must resign my job here effective May 30. I have learned a great deal in my time at the Blackbird, and I will miss the rest of the staff. However, I have been offered the opportunity to serve as a translator and editor for an organization in Indianapolis, and I believe this new position will best fulfill my professional goals.

Thank you for giving me the opportunity to work at the Blackbird. I am especially proud to have taken on some of the business responsibilities of ordering supplies and talking to vendors in addition to my bartending. I wish the Blackbird continued success in the future.

Sincerely,

[Edmund would sign his name here.]

Edmund Dantès

FIGURE 7: **Resignation letter.**

CHAPTER SUMMARY AND KEY POINTS

- Well-written professional correspondence places you in the same world as the employer, emphasizes your strongest qualities clearly and concisely, is memorable, and invites future contact.

- Customizing your cover letter is key to making a persuasive case for yourself.

- Rather than restating your resume, use your cover letter to connect the employer's needs to your own narrative of growth or accomplishment.

- When writing other professional correspondence, keep the reader in mind.

- Write an email as formally as you would a traditional letter.

CHAPTER SIX

INTERVIEWING

"Many attempts to communicate are nullified by saying too much." – Robert Greenleaf

INTRODUCTION

You are sitting across the room from a candidate you've brought in to interview for an open position at your organization. As the hiring manager, you know you have to make a big decision as to whether this person brings the right combination of experience, skills, values, and interests and would be the best fit for the organization. You also know that, in addition to salary and benefits, the cost of hiring and training the employee make the gravity of the situation stronger. Plus, every day the position goes unfilled, the organization is losing productivity or unable to provide services. You have very little evidence—a 45-minute interview, a resume and cover letter, and perhaps a few 5-minute conversations with references who may be biased toward the candidate—upon which to base your decision. You don't really know this person, the quality of their work, or their productivity level.

LEARNING OBJECTIVES

- Develop an interview mindset that focuses on the employer's needs and concerns but is also sensitive to the mutual purpose of the process

- Understand the importance of preparation for an interview

- Know about different interview settings, types of interviews, best practices for verbal and nonverbal communication

- Be able to answer all types of questions using appropriate tactics and rules of interviewing

- Know how to dress appropriately and plan for the logistics of an interview

Is *this* person *the* person?

Interviewing can be just as scary and daunting for the interviewer (the employer) as it is for the interviewee (the job seeker). One often thinks of the pressures and anxieties of being interviewed: Did I answer the question "right?" Did I say too much—or too little? Did I include *everything*? Am I smiling? Am I making good eye contact? Do they like me?

But the interviewer, too, is grappling with internal questions and feels similar pressures and anxieties. Just as you, the interviewee, might feel you have a lot at stake, so does the interviewer.

So what makes an interview a good interview? The purpose of an interview is to get the job, so the answer is deceivingly simple: a good interview is one that convinces the interviewer that you can not only do the work, but can contribute to the mission and culture of the organization and be a worthwhile investment of the organization's resources.

This means that, in order to be successful in an interview, you must not only know yourself well and have a thorough understanding of the industry, organization, and position, but also place yourself in the role of the employer. By approaching the interview and answering questions in this mindset, you can better equip yourself to address the employer's needs, thereby increasing the chance that you will be offered the position. This chapter will explain the basics of interviewing, from preparation to dressing appropriately, while helping you develop a think-employer mindset.

PREPARATION

Research is critical to interview preparation, just as it is with resume and cover letter writing. This includes self-knowledge (as described in CHAPTER 1) and knowledge about the industry and organization (CHAPTER 2). Though you already have (or should have) done plenty of research for the earlier stages of the job-search process, before you have an actual interview, you should review the research you completed previously, and possibly even do additional in-depth research to prepare for the interview part of the process.

Research is important for a number of reasons. Researching the industry and organization allows you to speak intelligently and show the employer that you are interested in the field and have thought about yourself as a staff member within the organization. Like you, every organization has interests, values, and a particular set of skills that are useful. A good fit for the organization is a person who brings the right combination of skills, values, interests, and personality. As you are trying to show that you fit their needs, you can make progress toward this goal by demonstrating that you have thought about it.

Once you have used all the tools described to you in CHAPTER 2 to research the industry and organization, you should refer back to your self-knowledge in search of proof of the interests, values, and skills desired by the organization. The resume you submitted as part of your application for the position is a good place to start. Every experience and accomplishment statement has at least one story behind it that demonstrates a skill, expresses an interest, or highlights a value-based decision you have made. You should select specific examples from your experience that convey relevant pieces of information. Those examples may come from the resume, but you should also feel free to use other examples from your experience if they are relevant.

Interviewing is also about making a meaningful connection with the people who interview you; they are the ones who will be making the decision as to whether you will be brought back for another interview or offered a position with the organization. It is in your best interest to know as much as possible about the people who will interview you. What is their background? Where did they go to school? What position does each of them hold, and what are their responsibilities? Do they prefer ideas or are they more interested in facts? While you cannot know everything about a person, and you certainly don't want to stalk them, you can use resources like website biographies, online resumes, or even just scanning

MARKETING YOUR EDUCATION

All of your experience is marketable to potential employers. This includes your education. Students who obtain degrees from professional schools such as education or business schools often have no trouble talking about the most relevant aspects of their education, especially when they are related to the position for which they are applying. It is important to remember, however, that any degree or major can be worth marketing if it is done so appropriately.

Liberal arts students, and really all students, should think about the skills they have developed while taking a broad spectrum of courses. Think about specific course projects or presentations where you used skills such as written or verbal communication, analysis, or problem solving. The breadth of experience itself could be marketed in the right situation. Just remember, a degree is something that expands your career options and skill set, not something that limits them. Use it to your advantage in an interview.

Below is a list of questions that could be asked of the employer during an interview. But instead of asking these questions, use them—along with your research about the field and organization—as a guide in drafting your own questions to ask.

- Why is this position open now?

- Would you describe a typical day's activities?

- What personal characteristics are important for success in this position?

- To whom would I report?

- What are some of the organization's short-term goals? Long-term goals?

- What challenges does the organization face?

- What do you like about working for the organization?

- What is the next step in the hiring process?

the contents of the person's office (diplomas, pictures, etc.) to help you make a stronger connection during an interview. (See Activity 6.1 in the APPENDIX for assistance in preparing for the interview.)

Your research should also be used as you create questions to ask the employer. Interviewing is a two-way street. As much as the employer is interviewing you for the position, you are also interviewing them. And while the employer will lead the interview and ask most of the questions, it is important that you are prepared with appropriate questions when the interview is turned over to you. Your questions should be professional and focus on information you need to help you make a decision as to whether *this* position with *this* organization is a good fit for you. Your questions, however, should not broach areas of compensation or benefits or be so simplistic that they could have been answered through conducting a little research on your own. It is important to have questions—and have them written down—because if you do not ask questions, you may seem unprepared and disinterested in making sure you and the organization are a good fit. You should prepare written questions to ask during all stages in the interview process.

As a final step in your preparation, you should practice interviewing. This can be as simple as grabbing a friend to ask you some general interview questions or as involved as dressing up and completing a practice interview with a career advisor at your school's career center. If it all possible, it is a good idea to have your practice interviews recorded so that you can review them to see what you said and how you looked saying it. While many people are reluctant to do so because they are afraid of what they look or sound like, recording yourself can be one of the most powerful ways to understand what you are doing well and what could be improved while interviewing.

Whatever methods you use to practice interviewing, remember that interviewing is like anything else: the more you practice, the more comfortable you will be with the process. Riding a bike wasn't easy the first time; nor was reading; and neither was driving. The more you practiced them in the most realistic sense possible, the more comfortable and skilled you became at them. It is no different with interviewing.

INTERVIEW SETTINGS AND COMMUNICATION

The most common setting for an in-person interview is the location where you would work if you are hired. You may also encounter interviews in other settings, such as at a career fair, at your school's career center, via phone, or over lunch or dinner. Regardless of setting, good communication—both verbal and nonverbal—is imperative to a successful interview.

IN-PERSON INTERVIEWS

The in-person interview will likely be among the final steps in the hiring process. Think of every interview as your last chance to make a connection with the employer and prove, through your previous experience and ideas about the future, that you can do the job and contribute to the organization. The in-person interview is the ultimate demonstration of your verbal and nonverbal communication skills. If your communication skills are weak, your chances at having interview (and job-search) success will be greatly diminished—even in cases where your research, skills, and experience far exceed those of your competition.

The following are guidelines and best practices for verbal communication:

- **Use proper English.** Speak in a professional way. This means avoiding colloquial speech and slang (words and phrases such as "undergrad" and "ain't") and acronyms or abbreviations ("IU" vs. "Indiana University"). Most people will be unfamiliar with the abbreviated form of a name, so being clear by saying the entire name is better. You should also use correct grammar and appropriate language.

- **Avoid non-words and phrases.** Nearly everyone is guilty of using non-words and phrases. Whether it be "uhm," "like," or "you know," these fillers can easily become distracting to the employer and tend to show a lack of awareness about what you are saying. Too often, people are unaware that they are using non-words and phrases. The best way to determine whether you are using them is to record yourself, as mentioned earlier in the chapter, and listen to what you say. If you find yourself guilty of employing non-words and phrases, practice identifying your use of them so that you can avoid using them. As they are often used to fill time, realize it is acceptable to pause briefly on occasion while you try to find the appropriate word or phrase to use. Nerves, too, sometimes cause people who might not usually say non-words and phrases to utilize them during interviews.

- **Speak clearly and confidently.** In order for employers to appreciate your experiences and all you have to say, they have to be able to hear and understand you. Make sure you speak slowly enough so that every word you say can be heard. People who speak too quickly or too softly during an interview give the impression that they are uncomfortable, leaving the employer to wonder whether the discomfort stems from natural tendencies, nerves, or a lack of confidence with your experience or research. Speak with good diction, at a pace that is not rushed, and at a level that one can comfortably hear (but not too loud!). Doing so suggests that you have confidence in what you have to offer.

- **Know where your story is going.** Have you ever seen a sub-par movie or read a book where the story wanders aimlessly into side stories or ends without resolving the central issue? It's unsettling and anticlimactic. So don't let the same thing happen to you during an interview. Every word of every response counts and should add to the case of your candidacy. As was alluded to in the Greenleaf quotation that began this chapter, tangents will dilute your message. People tend to remember the last thing they heard, so statements that start strong but trail off or end abruptly or weakly equate to a poor response, while those that start weak and end strong may turn out to be a good response; the goal is to start strong, be strong, and end

DEALING WITH NERVES

Just about everyone is nervous in an interview and many find the process quite stressful. It often stems from uncertainty about the future and other things you can't control. Nervousness shows that the interview is important to you. So, in this regard, it is not such a bad thing. However, you do not want your nervousness to cause your interview performance to suffer.

The best tactic for minimizing nerves is to thoroughly prepare by doing your research and practicing. You will probably experience some nervousness no matter what, but if you can become aware of the problem and not allow it to take control, you stand a better chance of releasing the anxious feelings. While you do not want to recite rehearsed answers during an interview, you should have a good idea ahead of time about what you are going to say. If you know what you bring to the organization in terms of skills and experience and how that relates to the organization and position, you should be able to remain focused and work through the nervousness.

strong. Know the point of each response you give and finish it in a way that proves the argument you are trying to make. You should not be afraid to take a few seconds to collect your thoughts before answering a question to ensure you know what you want to say before you start speaking.

- **Listen.** Remember that communication goes both ways: as you talk, employers listen and as they talk, you listen. Interviewees often get caught up in thinking about their response before the employer has even finished the question. If you are not careful, you can end up responding in a way that misses the point of the employer's question. If you do not understand the question, you should ask the employer to repeat the question. But be cautious about doing this too much. Also, under no circumstance should you interrupt the employer while they are speaking, even if you know what they are saying or asking. Finally, make sure that you actually answer the question you were asked; listen to yourself, and repeat the question to yourself or out loud (by rephrasing) if it will help you remember it.

As for nonverbal communication:

- **Shake well.** Your interview will probably contain a number of handshakes. An effective handshake is one that is firm and lasts a reasonable amount of time—usually 2 or 3 shakes. You certainly don't want to hurt the employer by squeezing too hard, but neither do you want to extend a limp hand. A good handshake is accompanied by eye contact and a smile.

- **Make eye contact.** Eye contact is important in an interview. It shows confidence in what you are saying and suggests honesty and interest in the interview. On the other hand, staring at the employer can be even more unsettling than making little or no eye contact.

- **Posture yourself.** You should sit up straight with relaxed shoulders and good posture. Lean slightly forward on occasion to show interest, but avoid leaning backwards as it tends to show disinterest or over-confidence. Keep your body language open and avoid crossing your arms. Nodding in agreement with something the employer has to say, as well as subtle hand gestures and movements are okay, but don't be erratic. Also try not to fidget, play with your pen, or move your legs up and down. And be aware of chairs that swivel or move back and forth. You want the attention to be on what you have to say and not what you are doing.

- **Smile!** Don't underestimate the power of a smile. Not only is it a pleasant thing to see, but it suggests to the employer that you are friendly and happy to be there. Remember the interview is about fit, and rarely do unhappy people "fit in." Ultimately, it is about letting your true self shine through and preventing your nerves from obscuring who you really are.

Verbal and nonverbal communication are equally important when it comes to the in-person interview. No one likes conflicting messages. An interview where a candidate speaks effectively but demonstrates poor posture and a lack of friendliness suggests someone who could probably do the work but might not fit in with the organization. The result: the employer moves on to another candidate. If you don't treat each interview as if it were your final interaction with that employer by using your research to say and do the right things, it will likely be your last interview with that employer.

PHONE INTERVIEWS

Phone interviews are challenging. They are often used as screening interviews because using them is a cost-effective way for employers to identify the strongest candidates for advancement in the hiring process, though they can be used at any point in the process. Phone interviews are usually shorter than in-person interviews and provide the added challenge that you cannot see the employer and their reactions to what you are saying, and they cannot see you. Because of this, it can be more difficult to make a personal connection with the employer. Because the visual piece of the discussion is missing, keep your answers on the short side so you do not lose the employer's interest. Do not be so brief as to look unprepared, thereby failing to advance your cause; but you should also avoid responses that go much beyond a minute or two.

The phone interview will usually take place in a setting more comfortable to you, which, ironically, can be a disadvantage if not approached properly. Ensure that your environment is conducive to engaging in an interview. Anything that may cause a distraction should be removed; this includes shutting off the computer, television, or a second phone that might ring, temporarily relocating pets, and sending roommates, family, or friends elsewhere until the interview is finished. Isolate yourself so you can concentrate on the employer and your mission of presenting yourself and experiences in the best way possible. You should avoid using a cell phone unless you are certain the reception will be adequate, the call will not be dropped, and your battery will last through the entire conversation. If you are interrupted, it is in your best interest to acknowledge the interruption to those who are interviewing you, apologize for it, and try to move on from it as quickly as possible.

Ultimately, you want to treat the phone interview as if it is an in-person interview. You probably wouldn't smoke or chew gum (and one shouldn't) during an in-person interview and you shouldn't in a phone interview either. Make sure you have a copy of your resume in front of you. You should do all the things, even the "nonverbals," during a phone interview that you would during an in-person interview, including smiling. You might even gesture lightly with your hands as you normally would in a conversation. Consider standing so that you project more energy. Write down the names of the people who are interviewing you so that, in lieu of eye contact, you can use their name to make a personal connection with them. Your goal is to make your phone interview as personable as possible and convince the employer to invite you to take part in the next step of the hiring process.

CAREER FAIR INTERVIEW

The interaction you have with an employer at a career fair is essentially a screening interview. Lasting just a few minutes, the conversation is your opportunity to make a good first impression with a recruiter who is charged with bringing in the best candidates to compete for a limited number of job openings. This mini screening interview should be treated like an in-person interview, but with the focus of a phone interview. You have a small amount of time to convey to the recruiter that you have skills and experiences worth discussing further.

DINING INTERVIEWS

Part of your interviewing experience may involve dining or cocktails. This could be part of the formal interview process or termed as an informal gathering. Regardless, it is important to remember that until you are offered and have accepted the position, you are always a candidate and in the midst of the interviewing process. The focus will be on you, and your focus should remain on the employer—not the food or entertainment! (This is your time to try to convince an employer you are *the* candidate, even if you are really hungry.) Use common sense when it comes to ordering; keep your meal light and order something that will allow you to continue to take part in the conversation without being distracting. Avoid alcoholic beverages, but if you do drink, be conservative and do not put yourself in a position to negatively impact your candidacy. It might be after hours and the person with the hiring authority might have gone home, but the interview is still taking place. It's always taking place while in the company of representatives from the organization.

TYPES OF INTERVIEWS

No matter what the interview setting, you will encounter one of three types of interviews. The one-on-one interview is typically the easiest to master. Since it is you and just one representative of the employer, you know where a connection needs to be made and whom to address as you answer. It is also clear that they have your undivided attention.

You may encounter an interview where you are interviewed by more than one person at a time. This many-to-one relationship is called a panel interview. It can be more difficult to make a personal connection when there is more than one person interviewing you, but this does not mean you shouldn't try. It is likely everyone in the room will take turns asking questions of you. When responding, start by speaking to the person who asked the question and during the course of your response try to connect and direct your answer to each person on the panel. Make sure that you end the question by focusing your attention on the person who asked it.

Group interviews are the most challenging. While we all understand that we will be competing with others for the job, the group interview makes this abundantly clear. A group interview is when you are interviewed in a group with other candidates for the same position by one or more employer representatives. In other words, it is a single interview experience in which there is a one-to-many or many-to-many ratio between interviewers and interviewees. Because you are witness to the responses from other candidates, and they are witness to yours, added stress and a consciousness about the competition can enter the interview. The focus of your attention, however, should be on your interview and really should be no different than how you would communicate with the employer if it were a one-on-one interview. This type of interview is somewhat rare, and is often found as a screening interview in customer service environments and those that require lots of teamwork. Preparation would be no different than other interview types, but you will want to remain neutral in the group setting and show the employer that you are naturally trying to involve everyone in the group.

ANSWERING QUESTIONS

The questions asked during an interview are intended to provide the employer with insight about how your past experience, along with your values, interests, skills, and personality align with the needs of the organization. You will likely be asked different kinds of questions throughout the interview. Knowing that you will have to answer questions right after they are asked can be daunting. But given proper research, you should be able to anticipate most of the questions that will be asked during the interview.

THE RULES

The rules that follow are intended to give you strategy when responding to a question during the interview. Each of them can be applied to nearly every response you give during the interview. If you remember nothing else from this chapter, remember these rules!

- **Examine intent.** As previously mentioned, questions asked of you in an interview are typically intentional. After each question is asked, briefly analyze it by asking yourself "What is really being asked?" Some questions are fairly straightforward and easy to understand, while others are more complicated and may have history and concerns encoded into them. Addressing the perceived intent of the question will allow you to give direction to your response.

  Take, for example, the general question of "Tell me about yourself." This is a simple question, but even it can be analyzed and reworked into more specific questions that can help you better answer it, alternately becoming "Who are you and why are you here?" The more complicated behavior-based question "Tell me about a time when you worked with a difficult coworker" has a lot more built into it. The question essentially concedes that there will, at some point, be conflict in the workplace, be it with another staff member or with a customer. So your goal is to assure them of your ability to prevent conflicts as well as manage them when they arise.

- **Tell a story.** A stranger walks up to you and says "I'm a good person who likes to have a lot of fun. You should be my friend!" Are you inclined to be their friend? Probably not. There is no context to the request, nor any actual proof that they are a good person, would make a good friend, share your interests, or would be fun to hang out with. If you knew a little bit more about the person, you probably still wouldn't be inclined to be friends with them just yet, but you might consider having lunch with them to explore the possibility.

Your responses in interviews need context too. Every response should contain a true story from your experience that highlights or proves what you are trying to say. This includes your responses to behavior-based questions where a story is explicitly requested, as well as other questions where the need for a story may not even be implied.

Several tools in the form of acronyms have emerged over the years to assist interviewees in telling their stories. SPAR—standing for Situation, Problem, Action, and Result—is the one we'll use in this text. The idea is that your response should describe a situation, the problem at hand, the action you took, and the result of your action. Again, it is just like a short story: there is a setting or exposition, a building action where the problems are encountered or laid out, a climax or turning point where action is taken, and some type of resolution where the results of the action are understood and evaluated. Because they are in direct relation to the action(s) you took, the results are the most important part of the story; make sure you adequately explain them as you finish your story.

- **Keep it relevant.** Whatever information you divulge or story you tell in an interview, keep it relevant to the position. One thing you never want to do in an interview is say something that can hurt your candidacy. The more you wander into discussing personal interests or experiences not related to the position, the more you increase the chances that you say something you wish you hadn't. And once it has been said, it can't be taken back. Good research and common sense will help you establish the boundaries of talking points within an interview.

- **Be positive.** You should remain positive at all times during the interview. Even when you are discussing an experience that you found to be negative, you should frame it in a positive way or avoid discussing it at all. This is especially true when talking about people for or with whom you have worked. No one wants to work with a negative person and if you portray negativity, you will undoubtedly cast yourself as one. This concept of being positive also extends to questions that directly target negative aspects. For example, when asked about a weakness or challenge, acknowledge the negative, but immediately move to the positive by explaining how you plan to improve the weakness, or give examples of overcoming a previous weakness.

LOST WITH ONE QUESTION: *MONICA'S INTERVIEW*

Up until this point, the interview had gone well—really well. Monica answered all the questions the panel asked with poise. She had done her research. She made sure she had good eye contact with each person on the panel, gave concrete examples of her skills, and demonstrated her knowledge of the field. All three of the committee members were clearly impressed by Monica's responses and, had the interview ended at that moment, they would most certainly have hired her.

But the committee asked a few more questions before turning the interview over to Monica for her to ask any questions she had.

"Tell me about your worst boss," Sheila, the head of the department and committee chair, asked. Without even thinking about it, Monica responded by recalling an experience she had with the supervisor at her internship two years earlier. She told the panel about how poorly she was treated, especially compared to the other interns. Her boss gave Monica all the boring tasks to do, sent her home for no reason some days, and made her stay late other days to enter figures into a database. Recalling the experience to the committee was making the soon-to-be college graduate upset.

Though it was clear that the committee members were uncomfortable, she couldn't stop herself. As she continued her response—which only lasted a minute or so—it was also becoming clear to Monica that what the committee really wanted to know was how she worked with people with whom she might not get along and what she learned from working with or for difficult people in the past.

The interview ended soon after her outburst. As Monica reflected about the interview on her drive home she knew she had made some missteps at the end of the interview. Yes, the internship experience was awful, but she knew that she needed to show professionalism. She shared too much information, especially irrelevant information. She was so negative. She failed to recognize what was really being asked of her.

Monica told herself to be realistic about the job, but remained hopeful that an offer might come despite what had happened in the interview. The committee, however, knew otherwise; all it took was one question.

TYPES OF QUESTIONS

There are five broad categories of questions that you may encounter during the interview process. Many employers use a combination of types of questions during the course of a single interview. The five question types are general, behavior-based, case-study, testing or stress, and off-the-wall. Knowledge of the types can help you to strategize your responses, as each tries to get at different aspects of your qualifications and ideas. (See Activity 6.2 in the APPENDIX for sample interview questions from these categories.)

- **General questions.** General questions are typically open-ended questions that allow you flexibility in your talking points for the response. Because of this, it can be difficult to gauge what the employer is looking for in a response, and you are more susceptible to accidentally divulging irrelevant information. Nearly every interview will begin with a few of these, the most common ones being *Tell me about yourself*, *What strengths do you bring to the position*, and *What is your greatest weakness*? Though specific examples are not explicitly asked for, remember to tell a story (or stories) when answering general questions by using the SPAR technique.

- **Behavior-based questions.** The belief that past behavior is a good predictor of future behavior is the underpinning of behavior-based questioning in an interview. With questions of this type, an employer will ask you to talk about a time in the past where you have encoun-

TELL ME ABOUT YOURSELF

It's usually the first question you get in the interview, and for that reason it is among the most important. It sets the tone of your interview and, if answered well, can set the direction of the questions and answers that follow. You might think of your response as an extended thesis statement that establishes what experiences and skills make you the most qualified candidate. Let's first look at a bad example:

> "Well, my name is Nichole, and I'm 22 years old and I'm from Fort Wayne. I have a brother and a sister, three nephews, one niece, and a cat. I love politics and travel, and right now I'm looking for a job."

See any problems? They are numerous:

- Name: they know it.
- Age: they can ballpark it by looking at you; plus it's irrelevant.
- Hometown: probably not relevant here either.
- Quantity of family members: so what?
- Hobbies: unrelated to the job means it's unimportant to the recruiter.
- Looking for a job: they might have guessed.

The problem with the response wasn't that Nichole said anything particularly bad—it's just that she didn't really say anything at all. So, if this is the wrong way to answer, what's the right way? In an interview, time is precious. Prior to your interview, think of a few things you want the recruiter to remember about you after you leave the room. Sell yourself! See what you think of this answer:

> "I'll be graduating in May with honors, with a double major in economics and international studies. I have consistently advanced in my part-time job at (Organization A) while attending school full time, and I've held three leadership positions in my sorority. And, right now, I'm finishing up my internship with

the Department of State. Accomplishing all of this hasn't been easy, but I've certainly honed my skills in time management, organization, and leadership. That's a good thing, because I feel completely ready to enter the workforce, and excel in helping (Organization B) achieve goals in (x, y, and z)!"

Here, Nichole is focusing on achievements, accomplishments, and transferable skills, while connecting all of this to the organization. In other words, she is focusing on things that are important to the potential employer. In an interview situation where time is limited and first impressions count for so much, preparation is essential. Prepare your sales pitch ahead of time and keep the interview focused on your highlights from beginning to end!

tered or accomplished something. These are the very questions for which the SPAR technique, described above, was invented—so make sure you employ it. You'll know it's a behavior-based question if it begins with something like "Tell me about a time..." As you answer the question, make sure you focus on the action you took and the results of that action, as these are the most important aspects when it comes to behavior-based questions.

- **Case-study questions.** You may encounter questions where you are read aloud or are asked to read a scenario, after which you are asked a question or a series of questions. These are called case-study questions. While there will probably be right and wrong answers, the intent of this type of questioning is usually to better understand your thought process. Thus, it is important you understand the scenario and that you explain how you reached your conclusion or what led you to make a particular set of recommendations.

- **Testing or stress questions.** With testing questions, the employer wants to see how you react in uncomfortable situations. This type of question is most often used for positions where you may encounter high-stress situations on occasion. While there is usually an honest underlying inquiry into something from your past, the focus is often more on your affect and ability to remain professional. Less intense forms of this question type might include *Why is your GPA so low?* or *Why were you not more involved in school?* Positions that are high in stress will often involve interviews with numerous testing questions, environments or situations that do not foster calmness (such as those where there are lots of interruptions or noise), and pressure to answer quickly or vigorously defend your responses— challenging your ability to remain calm and poised. It is imperative for those who might encounter this type of interview to practice in such environments as much as possible.

- **Off-the-wall questions.** Off-the-wall questions are questions that are, at best, tangentially related to the position for which you are interviewing. They are usually asked toward the end of an interview with a couple of goals in mind. Because they are often unrelated to the position, it's difficult to see them coming, so employers ask them to see how you react to the unexpected. It also gives them a glimpse into your personality from a different vantage point. The best responses tend to be honest and humorous while managing to find some point of connection between the candidate and the position. Common questions include *If you could have any person (living or dead) to dinner, whom would it be and why?* or *Which character from a recent movie best personifies you and why?* With questions like these, the "why" is important, even if it is not explicitly asked.

INAPPROPRIATE QUESTIONS

While there are technically no illegal questions, there are questions that are inappropriate. Inappropriate questions are those that broach the topics of your nationality, ancestry, marital status, race or color, religion, sexual orientation, physical disabilities or handicaps, pregnancy, birth control, child care, or number of dependents. What is illegal, however, is when employers make decisions based upon any of the above factors, as it usually puts them in violation of federal or state laws.

If you find yourself in a situation where you are asked an inappropriate question, you have a few options. You could, of course, just answer the question if you feel comfortable doing so. As with your responses to all questions, you should examine the intent of the question. Most inappropriate questions are asked because the person conducting the interview is unaware of the potential to misuse—illegally—the information. If you can determine what the reason for asking the question is, you have yet another option: to address the underlying issues of the question without actually answering the direct question.

Other options include ignoring the question and simply (and perhaps awkwardly) just talk about something else that is relevant to the position or refusing to answer. The latter will probably not bode well for your candidacy, but you probably don't want to work for an organization that prioritizes such things anyway. This also suggests your last option—ending the interview yourself. This is something you should probably only employ if you know the question was very intentional or if you have tried one of the previous tactics to avoid answering to no avail.

APPEARANCE AND LOGISTICS

Once you have an in-person interview scheduled, you are going to need to look professional and know how to get to the interview site. Most will find this to be common sense, but some will not take all the necessary steps to plan appropriately in order to ensure their appearance enhances their candidacy and to prepare for all the logistical details that surround an interview.

INTERVIEW ATTIRE AND APPEARANCE

Nearly all employers agree that your attire and appearance have an effect on your candidacy. If you are not well-dressed or groomed, you give the impression that you are not really interested in or enthusiastic about the position—something that needs to be conveyed in the interview. Your appearance and attire should be conservative and at the very least be one level above what the people in the position you hope to obtain normally wear.

Because some people are very sensitive to colognes and perfumes, it is wise to avoid them altogether. Your clothes can say a lot about you, but you don't want them to speak for you. This is why conservative is best. It's also not about having expensive clothing. You just want to look nice and neat. Those who are interviewing for a position in fashion or a creative industry have a bit more flexibility, but caution should be exercised. Hair should be styled neatly, extraneous jewelry and

MEN

- A dark-colored suit

- Pressed shirt with complementary tie with a simple pattern or design

- Polished shoes

- No cologne

WOMEN

- Skirt and jacket or pant suit

- Polished, conservative shoes

- Minimal jewelry

- No Perfume

body piercings temporarily removed, and tattoos covered, where possible.

Be conservative and minimalistic in what you bring with you to the interview too. Women needing a purse should bring the smallest one possible, containing only what they might need during the interview process. Both men and women should avoid bringing bags or briefcases. All that is usually needed is a pad of paper (usually contained within a faux leather folder, sometimes called a padfolio) where you can keep your notes and questions for the interview, take notes during the interview process, and store copies of your resume, references, and a pen. Simple is better.

Planning of your attire and what you bring will likely help you feel more prepared and less stressed. Nothing is worse than being unable to find the matching shoe or sock, realizing at the last minute that your suit was not dry cleaned after its last use several months ago, or being unable to produce an extra copy of your resume when requested by the employer because you forgot it at home.

GETTING TO THE INTERVIEW SITE

You also need to plan how you get to the interview. Being late for an interview is one of the best ways to terminate your candidacy. As far in advance as possible, try to obtain an interview itinerary that outlines where, with whom, and at what time you will meet with the representative from the organization. Familiarize yourself with it and use it as a tool for your research and interview preparation.

If you are traveling a medium distance and the employer is not providing a place for you to stay the previous night, you might consider arriving early and getting a hotel at your own expense if you can afford it. If you are traveling a long distance, you will usually have most traveling expenses paid for by the employer, and they may even handle some of the arrangements for you. It is important to understand the traveling terms before proceeding with making any travel plans.

On the day of the interview, give yourself plenty of time to get there, even if it means waiting in the car or walking around the block for a while because you are early. This is especially true for interviews that take place locally; you cannot accurately predict traffic patterns and travel issues no matter how much experience you've had with the area. You might even consider a test run the day before the interview if the location is unknown to you.

CHECKING IN AND THE INTERVIEW ITSELF

While you definitely do not want to be late to arrive at the interview site, you also do not want to be too early. Try not to be more than 10 minutes early to an interview. Being too early might make the employer feel as if they have to entertain you and also gives you the opportunity to sit and over-think the interview you are about to enter.

Think of the interview as starting the moment you pull into the parking lot of the interview site. Anyone with whom you exchange glances, nod to, or cut off in the parking lot might have influence in the hiring decision. This is true of receptionists, interns, and administrative assistants you may encounter once arriving on site. Keep things upbeat, cordial, and pleasant.

When it comes time to migrate to the interview room, remember to shake the hand of everyone you meet. You'll also want to let the person conducting the interview lead the way to the interview location and let them dictate the seating if it isn't clear when you walk in the room. The walk to the interview room will probably involve some trivial conversation about the weather or other topics. Keep things positive and don't say anything that could hurt your candidacy.

As mentioned in previous sections, the interview itself will consist of a variety of questions. Remember the rules and demonstrate that you have good verbal and nonverbal communication skills. Many employers find their ideal interview to be a conversational one, so if it moves in that direction, go with it. This also means that your points should be well thought out and stories used to support arguments in a way that it is not so obvious you are using interviewing techniques to help you move through the experience. Additionally, if you have developed a professional portfolio for the position, the interview is an opportune time to introduce it and reference specific examples of your relevant work.

ENDING THE INTERVIEW

The end of the interview will usually be signified by the question "Is there anything else we should know about you?" After responding, the interview will be turned over to you to ask your questions—something that you should have prepared. If any questions were answered during the course of the interview, don't ask them. If new questions emerged, hopefully you wrote them down at some point when you had a free second. Make every effort to ask intelligent questions and if the employer's response offers an opportunity for you to make a connection to one of your relevant skills, interests, or experiences, feel free to capitalize on the opportunity.

Don't forget to ask about the next step in the process before leaving the interview. And, of course, thank your interviewers and shake hands in appreciation once again as you leave.

AFTER THE INTERVIEW

Immediately following the interview you should congratulate yourself—you got through it! Take a few minutes to reflect upon what you did well and the case you made for yourself as a candidate. Also think about how you fit in with the organization. Can you see yourself working there for a few years, with those people, in that environment? As you look forward to other potential interviews, were there opportunities you missed? Did you communicate effectively? Ask yourself what can be improved for the next time... as there will undoubtedly be a next time, be it next week or in a few years, when you go for a promotion or different job. (See Activity 6.3 in the APPENDIX for guidance in reflecting about an interview.) Finally, don't forget to send a thank-you letter or email within 24 hours of the interview (see CHAPTER 5). This is your chance to remind the employer of your unique skills, experiences, and ideas and affirm your continued interest in the position.

CONCLUSION

Interviewing is the ultimate step to securing employment and an exercise in both verbal and nonverbal communication. But while the style of interviewing is important, the substance is paramount. Employers are seeking to hire a candidate who brings the right skills, values, interests, personality, experiences, and ideas to the position. Proper research and preparation will help you to realize if and how you are that person so that you may effectively communicate it to the employer. Be prepared to answer a variety of types of questions in a variety of settings, providing answers that get to the heart of each question by telling a story that is both positive and relevant to the position. But do not forget that you are simultaneously interviewing the employer, and if you are offered the position, the final decision as to whether you are a good fit lies with you.

CHAPTER SUMMARY AND KEY POINTS

- The better your research about the industry, organization, position, people who will be interviewing you, and yourself, the more likely you will be able to say something meaningful in an interview.

- Good verbal and nonverbal communication will allow you to present yourself and your ideas in a professional and convincing manner.

- Regardless of whether you are being interviewed in person, via the phone, at a career fair or event, or while dining, be ready to answer general, behavior-based, case-study, testing or stress questions, and off-the-wall questions.

- Follow the rules of examining the intent of each question, telling a story in each response, and keeping your answers positive and relevant.

- Dress appropriately for the interview and remember that each person you meet or speak with may have some influence in your hiring.

- As you are being interviewed to see if you are good fit for the position, you are interviewing the organization to see if it is a good fit with you as well.

CHAPTER SEVEN

THE BUSINESS OF MONEY

"I'm living so far beyond my income that we may almost be said to be living apart." – E.E. Cummings

"My problem lies in reconciling my gross habits with my net income." – Errol Flynn

INTRODUCTION

These quotations by a renowned poet and legendary actor reflect the universal truth that most people can be challenged by their relationship to money—even the famous and well-connected. In the following pages, we'll tackle this subject by first demystifying the principal method for managing one's money—budgeting—and learn how this oft-dreaded process is not only uncomplicated, but also tremendously useful to you as a job seeker. From there we will look at the final piece of the formal job search: negotiating a job offer for the best possible pay and benefits.

BUDGETING BASICS

Knowing how much money you need for a realistic standard of living before applying for a job is as

LEARNING OBJECTIVES

- Appreciate the usefulness of budgeting before the job search

- Understand the fundamentals of budgeting—expenses, debt, savings, net income

- Know how to establish a basic monthly budget

- Recognize the importance of tracking expenses and sticking to your budget

- Be able to identify the three aspects of job offer evaluation and negotiation preparation

- Understand the basic skills and process of negotiating a job offer

important as meeting your potential in-laws before you get married (especially the ones that live nearby!)—it provides you critical information as to how your daily life will be impacted by your decision.

How will you know what your minimal salary requirements are, if you don't take the time to figure out how much money you need? You won't. And if you're planning to find work in a different city, you'll have an additional factor to consider. If you live in a small college town you may think the cost of living is high enough as it is, but if you move to Chicago or Paris it's going to be even higher, and you'll need to seek a correspondingly higher salary.

A budget is also an opportunity to give concrete expression to your values (as discussed in CHAPTER 1). By intentionally choosing to save, or to pay off debt, or to spend, you are consciously connecting your valuable life energy—which you are exchanging for money through your work—to what is most important to you.

The word "budgeting" is loaded with connotations, and to many people it sounds dreadfully boring. Isn't budgeting something that only misers who don't know how to have a good time worry about? No. Keeping a budget is as advantageous as referring to a map while driving in an unfamiliar area—while there may be occasional roadblocks that challenge you, in the long run you're much more likely to steer your financial life to your chosen destination. And while many people who have an aversion to numbers also fear budgeting, it actually requires no more than the simplest grasp of math.

EXPENSES

A basic monthly budget includes information about several areas, and one of the most important is your expenses. These include what you will pay each month for housing, utilities, food, transportation, insurance, personal care, entertainment, and clothing. If you are moving to a new location, search online for a "cost of living comparison" website to get a sense of how your expenses may differ.

SAVINGS

Savings is an essential realm of personal finance. By establishing accounts for larger goals such as a trip to Europe or a new car, your savings can be a direct expression of what you value or desire. Not to mention that it can be tremendously satisfying to see your money accumulate over time! Unfortunately, though, Americans have some of the lowest savings rates in the developed world, and millions of us end up paying huge amounts of interest for purchases we could have bought much cheaper if we'd saved for them. Others lose control of their finances entirely and go bankrupt.

Personal finance experts recommend that you save three to twelve months' living expenses for emergencies. How much you choose to save depends on multiple factors including your job security, the state of the economy, the job outlook for your field, and dependents you may be supporting.

DEBT

Debt is something that most college students are all too familiar with. Like many students, you may possess one or more credit or merchant cards. While using such cards in moderation can help you to establish a credit history, they can become a problem if you begin spending money you don't have. Even if you do have the money, cards often bear exorbitant interest rates and late fees that result in your paying significantly more for an item than if you had paid in cash. Credit cards are a big problem for many people, especially when they are starting out in the working world.

Yet, incurring debt is not always a bad thing. *Good debt* includes debt incurred for educational expenses (whew!) and for other assets that may appreciate in value or expand your income opportunities, such as real estate or a small business. *Bad debt* is debt incurred for items that depreciate in value or have little or no value after you purchase them, such as clothing,

The power of compound interest is that it earns you money on the money you're earning. Compound interest is especially effective over time. The following chart shows how much money you'd have at the age of 62 if you were to diligently put away $300 every month into an 8% interest-bearing account, beginning at age 42, 32, or 22.

Age at which you begin saving:	Total accumulated by age 62
Age 42	$176,706
Age 32	$447,108
Age 22	$1,047,302

vacations, living expenses, or a car. (Yes, even though having a monthly car payment may be as common as incurring a mortgage for a home, that doesn't make it good debt. If you do borrow money for a car, you'll end up paying significantly more for it "down the road.")

It's worth avoiding bad debt if at all possible. If you have some bad debt (which often has the highest interest rates), it's wise to take stock of your situation, as it may significantly impact your salary requirements and your resulting job search strategy. A formula for knowing your *debt danger ratio* is:

$$\textit{total bad debt owed} \div \textit{annual income} = \textit{debt danger ratio}$$

A ratio above 25 percent is in the danger zone, because interest on your debt can add to what you owe beyond your ability to repay it. Be careful; if you must go into debt, make sure it's good debt, not bad.

NET INCOME

Your take-home pay after taxes are withheld constitutes your net income. (Taxes will likely include federal, state, and social security taxes, and possibly others depending on your location.) Once you've established your monthly budget, and know what you'll need for expenses, savings, and debt repayment, you'll have a good idea of the monthly net income you'll need.

The salary amount you will agree upon with your employer is your *gross income* (your total salary *before* taxes are withheld). So how do you figure out what this amount should be in order to arrive at an appropriate net income? A reasonably accurate estimate can be obtained by using an online tax calculator. A good calculator will allow you to input a geographical location and an estimated gross salary, and use that information to calculate what your approximate net income would be. You may even be able to find a calculator that will estimate a gross salary based on a desired net amount. Just keep in mind that without the assistance of a professional tax expert, the number you come up with will be an estimate.

As you estimate your budget, don't make the mistake of thinking that *you* are the special one who will land the big job with the big salary, and that budgeting is unnecessary, or even beneath you. Do it anyway, estimating your anticipated salary on the low end. If you *do* get the big job, you'll be pleasantly surprised the next time you check your budget.

ESTABLISHING A MONTHLY BUDGET

Most of the time and effort spent developing a monthly budget takes place up-front, as you establish and test a system that will work for you. While it's important to regularly take time to make your system work for you, this shouldn't amount to more than a few hours per month.

Since your initial budgeting goal is to know how much money you will need in order to determine your salary requirements, it's important to gather as much information as possible, while recognizing that your budget will increase in accuracy over time. If you're not sure what a given expense will be, err on the side of overestimating it. Also, keep economic trends in mind, and if you'll be moving, factor in the cost of living at your new location.

Below is an example of budget categories, including places to track savings and debt repayment for multiple items, and several categories for expenses.

NET INCOME	$	EXPENSES			
SAVINGS		Communication		Personal (cont'd)	
Car maintenance	$	Cell phone	$	Health club dues	$
Emergency fund	$	Internet	$	Laundry/Dry cleaning	$
Insurance premiums	$	Food		Personal care	$
Medical/Dental	$	Groceries	$	Other	$
New car	$	Restaurants	$	Transportation	
Vacation	$	Housing		Fuel	$
Other	$	Rent	$	Parking	$
TOTAL SAVINGS	$	Gas/Electricity/Water	$	Public transportation	$
DEBT REPAYMENT	$	Personal			
Car payment	$	Bars/Clubs	$	TOTAL EXPENSES	$
College loans	$	Clothes	$		
Other	$	Entertainment	$		
TOTAL DEBT REPAYMENT	$	Gifts	$	GRAND TOTAL (savings + debt repayment + expenses)	$

RECORDING IT

You have several options for recording your budget:

- Pencil and paper
- Spreadsheet software such as Microsoft Excel
- Personal finance software such as Quicken or Microsoft Money

Each has its pros and cons. If you want a more flexible and simple system, and would like to master the essentials of personal finance, creating your own budget with pencil and paper or spreadsheet software is probably best. On the other hand, most software programs offer powerful features such as the ability to link directly to your checking account. If you desire the features that software offers, you may wish to go that route.

To create your own budget, see Activity 7.1 in the APPENDIX.

FINE-TUNING IT

Your first budget will be a rough estimate, based on the best information you're able to gather. But in the long run, a budget is only as useful as the data that informs it, and keeping track of your actual expenses is as important as planning for them. One of the easiest ways to track expenses is to make a habit of saving every receipt, and once each week, recording all your expenses. At the end of the month, get out your calculator and compare your estimated expenses (planned monthly budget) with your actual expenses. Use this information to improve the accuracy of the following month's budget.

STICKING TO IT

Whether you use pencil and paper or the latest software, setting up your budget is the easy part. Sticking to it can be more daunting. Keeping receipts and tracking expenses on a weekly basis can help you see whether you are sticking to your budget in each category, or whether your spending habits are sticking it to you. If you need financial discipline, try the "envelope system," in which you use real

MONEY MANAGEMENT:
THE GOOD, THE BAD, AND THE UGLY

The Good: As a high school freshman, Brittany started working and saving money, and set herself the goal of saving $10,000 by graduation, a goal she almost achieved. As a result, she was able to pay upfront for a large chunk of her college tuition, since her parents didn't have the resources to help. While Brittany did take out some student loans in college, she also continued to work part-time, and managed to save for a spring break trip to the Caribbean in her junior year. But when her best friend Dawn tried to convince her to buy $300 designer swimwear for the trip, Brittany was unmoved. Brittany is about to graduate with less than $5,000 of good debt.

The Bad: In his senior year of college, Kevin bought a new car with no money down, because he wanted to celebrate his upcoming graduation. Kevin figured he'd be bringing in the dough soon enough, so why not? But a few weeks later Kevin's buddy Drew bought a set of wheels that put Kevin's to shame. Because he needed to have the best, Kevin sold his newly purchased vehicle, losing over $6,000 because it had depreciated the moment he drove it off the lot. He then bought the newer version of Drew's vehicle, amassing even more debt. After college the economy took a downturn and it took Kevin eight months to find a job. During that time he couldn't keep up with the payments, and had to sell his vehicle at an even bigger loss than the first one. Kevin is taking the bus to his new job, because he's out of a car—though he's still paying for one.

The Ugly: In her sophomore year at college, many of Taylor's friends moved from the dorm to the newest and coolest apartment complex in town (with a little help from their parents). Taylor's family wasn't that wealthy, but she desperately wanted to stick with her friends so she took out a personal loan to pay for an apartment at the same complex. She avoided getting a job so she could maintain a relaxed lifestyle like her friends, and also began borrowing for food and other basics. After Taylor maxed out her credit cards, she found new cards that didn't require immediate repayment. It became her dirty little secret. She wouldn't even invite her parents over when they came to town, claiming that her apartment was too messy, but she was really just afraid they'd say she was making a big mistake. When the payments on her various credit cards and other loans came due and started to add up, she finally gave in and took a part-time job in order to meet the

(continued)

MONEY MANAGEMENT *(continued)*

minimum payments. A few months later, Taylor finally found the nerve to look her financial picture in the eye, and was shocked: she had over $50,000 in bad debt, and it would take her over 40 years to pay it off at the rate she was going. Taylor is now seeing a financial counselor and is seriously considering filing for bankruptcy soon after graduation.

money instead of debit or credit cards. Place cash for each budgeting category in an envelope at the beginning of each month. When you run out of the money in an envelope, you are not allowed to "borrow" from another envelope. You're done spending in that category for the month.

YOUR MONEY BELIEFS

As suggested in CHAPTER 1, becoming aware of your beliefs about work and the job search can profit you personally. Taking time to explore your beliefs about money can profit you in the original sense of the word. By the time we become adults, most of us have at least a few disempowering beliefs about money, such as:

- I'm not good with money
- I'll never make enough money
- It's wrong to have a lot of money
- My math skills are not adequate for the purposes of budgeting
- I'm above making and thinking about money
- Keeping track of my money is difficult and takes too much time

What are *your* beliefs about money and personal finance? Making your beliefs conscious as described in CHAPTER 1, and letting go of the negative, disempowering ones, while cultivating positive beliefs in their place, can lead you to a place of deep satisfaction with money and personal finance.

Now that you've got budgeting under your belt, it's time to explore what happens when you hear the magic words from an employer: "We'd like to make you an offer."

THE BUSINESS OF NEGOTIATION

They want you for the job! A weight has been lifted from your shoulders. But while your first instinct may be to relax and celebrate with your friends, the job search process is not quite over. Every job offer has "terms"—the details of what the employer is offering you in exchange for your time and energy (also called the "compensation package"). While you can accept the initial offer, it is expected by employers that you will negotiate to improve the terms for yourself, even for entry-level positions. Though negotiating is not a requirement, you have nothing to lose, and quite possibly something to gain. The Latin root of the word "negotiate" means "not leisure." In other words, this is *business*, and negotiation is an accepted element of business transactions.

The word "negotiation" may bring to mind cutthroat bargaining, but there is no reason it can't simply be a friendly conversation between two parties who are seeking common ground. Since the employer has offered you the job, it's likely that they believe you are the best candidate. With that knowledge in mind, you can begin the negotiation process with the confidence that you have something worthwhile to offer the employer, and that they know it.

PREPARING FOR NEGOTIATION

You should be prepared for negotiation even before your first interview, as it is not impossible that you will be offered the job at the interview's conclusion. There are three general areas to consider when preparing to negotiate—yourself and your situation, the general career field and the specific organization that has offered you the job, and the terms that are likeliest to be negotiable.

EVALUATE YOURSELF AND YOUR SITUATION

Determining the compensation and other benefits (such as health insurance) that you need is an essential first step. If you've completed Exercise 7.1 in the APPENDIX, you have a good idea of what the cost of living will be in the employer's geographical area, and your personal salary requirements for living there.

Reflect on the specific skills and knowledge that you are offering and how well they match the employer's needs. If you believe you are an excellent match for the job description, then your value to the employer is likely to be higher, and you'll be able to negotiate from a stronger position. But if you believe that the employer has other excellent candidates to choose from, or that you still have a lot to learn about the position or field, you may want to lower your expectations about the outcome of the negotiating process.

Also consider how you found the job. A job seeker who has been recruited by the employer will have the most leverage during negotiation. But even if you discovered the opening through your own efforts, you may be able to negotiate certain aspects of the offer.

EVALUATE THE FIELD, ORGANIZATION, AND ECONOMY

After evaluating your own needs and what you have to offer, research the field in which you are applying to work, and the specific organization that has offered you the job. While you may have researched the field to some extent already, additional research may turn up valuable data for negotiation purposes. For instance, if you've been offered an entry-level position, look for the most recent data on entry-level salary ranges for that occupation, and information on benefits. Your school's career center or library will be able to help you find these resources. Informational interviews (see CHAPTER 2) are another way to acquire information on average salaries and benefits in your field. (Of course, you should ask your interviewee about salaries and benefits in the field generally, not about their personal salary.)

If you haven't yet thoroughly researched your prospective employer, take time to review the organization's literature and website. Talk to former employees or employees in similar organizations, if you can find them. Look for organizational projects, trends, and other information that may be relevant to your occupational interests and abilities, which can help you demonstrate how your value to them exceeds what they may already acknowledge.

Also take into account general economic trends, both nationally and locally, and the number of similar positions that are currently available. If jobs are scarce and the employer has received many applications from attractive prospects, you will have less room for negotiation. If the economy is strong and applicants were few, you may have more leverage.

CONSIDER WHAT'S NEGOTIABLE

When most people see the word "negotiation," they think money. While it's true that salary is often not negotiable for entry-level positions, there's no harm in trying to improve this aspect of the offer. But there are many other aspects of an offer that may be negotiable—in fact, most of them!

After completing the research suggested in this section, take time to reflect on yourself and your situation, and what you've learned about the career field, the organization itself, and the general economy. This should give you a good idea as to the strength of your position.

To compare your values and goals to a job offer, see Activity 7.2 in the APPENDIX.

THE NEGOTIATION PROCESS

WHEN TO BEGIN

If you've been offered the job, in a sense you've already begun the informal negotiation process, for it started at your interview when you expressed why your experience and skills make you the best candidate for the position. Of course, you didn't discuss salary or other aspects of the job offer at the inter-

---

NEGOTIABLE OR NOT?

OFTEN NEGOTIABLE

- Salary
- Starting Date
- Moving Expenses
- Vacation
- Professional Development Funds
- Early Performance Evaluations
- Flex Time
- Workspace
- Performance Bonuses
- Geographic Location
- Office Space
- Parking
- Housing Allowance
- Travel Allowance
- Stock Options
- Company Car
- Retention Bonuses
- College Tuition Reimbursement

NOT NEGOTIABLE
- Health Plans
- Retirement Plans

view (and you never should). But once an employer makes you a job offer, the formal process can begin.

If that offer has been made verbally at first, ask to have it put in writing, which makes it more tangible and binding. Ask the employer for a decision date that will give you enough time to make an informed choice.

Always allow the employer to bring up the subject of compensation first. Obviously, you won't want to demand a certain salary or other terms before you know what is being offered. The employer's terms may be more generous than you were thinking of suggesting! Also, be sure to complete your research on average salary ranges before negotiating compensation, or you will risk asking for a higher amount than is reasonable or typical, making yourself seem inexperienced or presumptuous.

TO ACCEPT OR NOT ACCEPT

When you receive a job offer, you may feel an inner pressure to accept it right away. But most employers understand that it will take time for you to evaluate their offer, just as it took them time to select the best candidate from their pool of applicants. So don't allow yourself to succumb to the temptation of accepting the first offer that comes your way without evaluating it thoroughly. If you accept an offer right away, you lose your chance to negotiate, and all your leverage along with it. It's not acceptable to ask to change the terms *after* accepting an offer, so it's worthwhile to take time to review it thoroughly and compare it to the results of your research.

WALK-AWAYS AND COUNTEROFFERS

If you do decide to negotiate, you will typically begin by making a counteroffer. But before doing so, consider all the points you wish to negotiate, and your "walk-away" for each (the point at which you will decline to accept the job). While you can seek to improve the offered terms without planning to walk away if the employer will not improve upon them, your negotiation may be more effective if you *are* willing to walk away. The employer will sense that you mean business and that you take yourself seriously.

It is best to negotiate with someone who has decision-making power. If you are not negotiating with such a person, the process may take longer than you would like. If this happens, you may be tempted to communicate directly with the decision maker, but you will be better off respecting the employer's choice of staff for the process.

Be willing to reveal what you really need. The negotiating process can accelerate if you lay your cards on the table. For example, if the employer understands that your personal situation necessitates that they pay your moving expenses so that you can take the job, that information may encourage them to find a way to make that happen.

However, while it's best to be candid about your needs, don't take the negotiation process personally. Remember, business is business, and the outcome of the negotiation process does not reflect on you personally.

It's best to begin by negotiating the terms on which the two of you are most likely to come to agreement. Once the employer comes to agreement on one or two terms, they may be more likely to come to agreement on the remaining terms, in order to close the deal.

Be specific in what you ask for, and begin by asking for more than you would be willing to accept. By doing so, you'll be able to "come down," thus appearing to concede your position, which will make it easier for the employer to offer a concession as well. As an example, say you've discovered that the average annual entry-level salary range for your position is $30,000 to $40,000. The employer has offered you $26,000, but you've decided that you will walk away if they will not give you at least the minimal salary in the average range ($30,000). You begin by asking for $35,000, pointing out the average salary data you've discovered. The employer counters by offering $28,000. You lower your counteroffer to $33,000. Finally, the employer raises their offer to $30,000 and you accept.

If the employer states that a specific term is not negotiable, it's reasonable to ask if this is an absolute rule. Have they *never* negotiated this point with another person? If your position is strong, you may be able to bring such points into the negotiation.

As you negotiate, keep the employer's needs foremost in mind. Remind them of your skills and accomplishments and why these demonstrate that you're the best person for this job. In fact, during the negotiation process you may have the invaluable opportunity to directly demonstrate many transferable skills that you discussed in your application, such as communication, analytical, and problem-solving skills, as well as demonstrate a professional demeanor.

If the negotiation seems to be heating up, remind yourself that you are simply engaged in a dialogue, and that you are each seeking a mutually beneficial agreement. If the employer is unwilling or unable to meet your minimal walk-away point for any term that is important to you, it is your option to walk away. Remember, at *any* point you have the option to accept the offer, walk away, or continue negotiating. The ball is in your court.

If you need extra time to evaluate the offer, you can write a stall letter, in which you acknowledge the employer's offer and ask for an extension of the decision date. You need not say why. Ask the employer for the time you need, but keep in mind that you may even have to negotiate *this* request! In the event the employer is pressuring you to make a decision and you're not ready to do so, you may want to reconsider whether they are the best fit for you. Also, bear in mind that there is a risk that asking for more time to decide could prompt the employer to withdraw the offer and choose another candidate. Anytime during this process, you may benefit from obtaining the opinion of a neutral party like a career advisor.

MAKING A DECISION

Negotiation can't go on forever, and soon enough it will be time to decide whether to accept the currently offered terms. This decision will depend on both external factors (your budget requirements, the standard salary for the occupation, and other relevant data you've uncovered) and internal factors (does it feel right to me? will I be satisfied if I accept the current offer as negotiated?). The best decision will come when you are willing to take all relevant factors into consideration, exploring the potential consequences of accepting or walking away.

If you decide to accept, do so not only verbally, but also in writing, stating the terms you've negotiated as you understand them (or instead, ask the employer to put the terms in writing). This is the best way to avoid possible misunderstandings and begin your new relationship with mutual understanding and clarity. If you choose to walk away, decline the offer graciously and diplomatically.

CONCLUSION

By taking the nominal time required to establish a monthly budget, you will have a thoughtful plan for connecting your values to your income, and possess essential information for prudently considering and negotiating job offers that come your way. The negotiation process is likely to be most effective when you take the time to research and reflect on yourself and the organization with which you are negotiating. The closer your skills and background match the needs of the employer, the more leverage you will have in negotiation. You can begin the formal process of negotiation by making a counteroffer for the terms that you would like to improve. At a certain point it will be time to decide whether to accept the currently negotiated terms, or to walk away from the offer. While you are not required to go through the negotiation process, if you do you will learn something about yourself, and quite possibly improve the terms that were initially offered to you.

CHAPTER SUMMARY AND KEY POINTS

- Knowing how much money you need to live on is essential information when applying for a job.

- A monthly budget should include categories for expenses, debt repayment, and savings.

- Recording expenses and sticking to your budget is as important as planning it.

- Exploring your money beliefs can empower your financial life.

- Negotiating an offer is a normal and acceptable part of the job search process.

- Prepare for negotiation by considering yourself and your situation, the general career field and the specific organization that has offered you the job, and the terms that are likeliest to be negotiable.

- While negotiating, keep the organization's needs foremost in mind, and remind them why you're the best person for this job.

CHAPTER EIGHT

TRANSITIONING FROM COLLEGE TO WORK

"Create a definite plan for carrying out your desire and begin at once, whether you are ready or not..."

— Napoleon Hill

INTRODUCTION

Your accumulated life experiences, including your education, activities, part-time jobs, internships, networking activities, and interviews have all led you here: your first professional job. What now? After spending most of your life in school, writing papers, preparing for exams, and listening to lectures, how will your life differ now?

While you will no longer be studying and writing papers, you may also no longer be living with your friends in the comfortable environment you are accustomed to. You have developed an identity as a college student. You know how to be a college student, and you are probably rather good at it by now. You've probably also worked hard to develop a network of friends and acquaintances with whom you study, work, socialize, and live. Giving up this familiarity and comfort in order to jump into an unknown

LEARNING OBJECTIVES

- Discover the significance of interpersonal relationships in the workplace

- Develop awareness of challenges and ethical dilemmas, and begin to construct methods for dealing with them

- Learn the importance of focusing on your primary work tasks

- Understand the consequences of verbal, nonverbal, and written communication in the workplace

- Recognize the value of professional development and mentors

world is intimidating, and perhaps even frightening. You're in the midst of a great transition in your life, and it is only natural that you may feel sad about what you are leaving behind, and overwhelmed at what lies in front of you. Consider talking about this with a family member, friend, or counselor. Your peers are likely feeling the same unease, so bringing it up with them might be helpful. Although the transition to work may be difficult, this can also be an exciting moment in your life; a time of growth and development, and a time to put your education to practical use and move into that "real world" that you've heard so much about.

As you make the transition from student to professional, you may believe that everything will now be different. After all, you have been a student all your life but you are a full-fledged adult now, working and interacting with other adults. Indeed many things will be different, but you may be surprised to find that other things will stay the same. After all, young or old, student or professional, people will be people; as long as you're dealing with human beings, similar patterns of group behavior will always exist. At the same time, however, every group is made up of different people and therefore has its own nuances. Thus, it may be more important for you to discover at this juncture how these particular people (your new colleagues) behave and how you will fit in with their preformed organizational structure, because fitting in will probably be your first step. Once you build your professional reputation by understanding your role and being effective in your work, you will earn the respect of your co-workers and then you may be able to effect change. In the meantime, take it slowly, and do your best to develop an understanding of the organization and its people. This may sound intimidating, but by taking a few simple steps toward understanding the structure and fitting into it, you may find that the transition will be positive and exciting.

Creating and maintaining your professional reputation throughout this process will be important, not only for your own satisfaction, but for your overall effectiveness in your first full-time position. Keep in mind that your reputation will follow you from job to job, and career to career, throughout your life. Your overall goal should be to develop a reputation as a positive, enthusiastic, effective professional. You may make some missteps along the way, but planning your approach and seeking plenty of assistance will likely help keep these to a minimum.

BUILDING EFFECTIVE PROFESSIONAL RELATIONSHIPS

Relationships are at the core of nearly everything we do as human beings. Our interaction with other people on a day-to-day basis teaches us, and those around us, a lot about who we truly are. How are you perceived? How do you handle encounters with other people? The answers to these questions will likely define how much you can accomplish within the organizational structure. You are about to embark on a new life in which you will spend at least 40 hours of your week with your colleagues. Indeed, roughly one-half of your waking hours will now be spent with one group of people. Of course, depending upon your field of employment, you may spend more or less time directly interacting with your colleagues; nonetheless, our professional relationships are important and often influential over our long-term success, no matter the work setting. People will begin to form opinions about you early on and your behaviors can add to, or detract from, the professional reputation that surrounds you.

GETTING TO KNOW YOUR NEW WORK "FAMILY"

Walking in the door on your first day facing a group of strangers who know each other, know their work, and know the organizational structure and politics, can be intimidating. An important thing to remember is that you will be a veteran member of this structure in due time; pace yourself in your efforts to fit in, and don't expect it to happen immediately. You are as unknown to them as they are to you. Think of it as similar to meeting the parents of a significant other. You know a little bit about them, and they know a little bit about you, but it's difficult to truly understand much about each other until some time passes. Remember, your primary reason for being there is to be effective in your work. Positive working relationships will certainly aid you in that effort, and poor working relationships will detract from it.

It is for these reasons, as well as your own long-term satisfaction, that you should ease into your new role and do so with careful observation. Observe the interactions of others in the workplace, and resist the temptation to share too many personal details in an effort to bond with your new colleagues. Generally speaking, jumping right into conversations that surround politics, religion, romantic dalliances, etc., will be frowned upon. As a new employee, focus more of your energy on diligently working, and finding common ground with your new colleagues, both in the work you do, and in your personal interests and preferences. If you're curious about something you see or hear, ask questions. The bonding will happen over time, if it is to happen at all. Being effective in your work will gain you more respect and therefore, more opportunities for positive interactions with your colleagues.

FRIENDS OR COLLEAGUES?

Social relationships with your colleagues can be a rewarding and important part of your adult life. In fact, if you have recently moved to a new location, your new co-workers may be the only people you know in the area. The primary difference between your interactions with colleagues and your interactions with friends is that colleagues must still be able to view you as a professional at work. Additionally, feeling as though your colleague is your "friend" can lead to frustration at work and simultaneously damage your overall interaction with that person. Perhaps a situation arises at work where you need that person's support; they do not provide support and, instead, argue against you. This can create both personal and professional disappointment, which can lead to resentment. This is not to say that you cannot, or should not, socialize with co-workers. In reality, that may be an integral part of the structure of your new workplace. You should, however, always view social functions with colleagues in the larger scope of your professional reputation. Minimize your risk of losing colleagues' respect by being careful what you say and do, and be aware that you have to continue to work with these individuals for some time. An employee who is not respected is very likely to be ineffective in the organization. Once your newness wears off, you will find these interactions to be more natural and comfortable. As with every part of this process, you need to allow yourself time to become one of the group.

POLITICS AND GOSSIP

Politics is, at its core, struggling and competing power structures resulting in decisions about who gets what, and how and when they get it. Office politics, just like any kind of politics, can contribute to an organization in a positive, effective manner; or it can be messy and detrimental to the organization's success and productivity. The first step in understanding your new office politics is to observe the various levels of politics at work around you, and then judge for yourself which ones are positive and which ones are negative. This takes time, keen observation, and patience.

Generally, organizations have a formal structure of power, made known via an organizational chart. The president, CEO, director, etc., is at the top, and the power trickles down from there. In reality, however, decisions may be made via a very different "chain of command." These informal power structures will be apparent in due time, if you are on the lookout. Certain employees, no matter where they fall on the organizational chart, will be more influential than their position implies. Who should you really go to when you need to get something accomplished? Who really makes the decisions? Awareness of these basic facts can expedite your progress, and cut through some organizational red tape. At the same time, a basic awareness of, and respect for, the formal structure is always expected.

One of the negative aspects associated with office politics is knowing or hearing the "dirt" on other people within the organization. Participating in such discussions can easily drag you into a spiral of office gossip, for which few have respect (though many do participate). This spiral often begins with innocuous intentions, and simply listening quietly as others gossip is generally the first step. From that point, it may become easier to spread the information that you hear. For many, this makes the awkward feeling of not fitting in dissipate a bit, and begins to aid

THE PRICE OF GOSSIP

Clint had been on the job a couple of weeks when his team went out for drinks after work. He quickly saw that his colleagues' conversation about Emily, a co-worker, just picked up where they left it off last time. None of it was positive and, in fact, it was rather disparaging. She was clearly the punch line of many of their jokes. In an effort to participate in the conversation, Clint chimed in with a story of something silly Emily recently said that no one else had overheard. They all laughed at her, and referred to her mistake as "yet another 'Emily' moment." Clint is now an instant hit at this gathering, but he leaves feeling guilty about his behavior. His bond with his team has seemingly strengthened, but at what personal cost to himself, and his own integrity?

the progress of feeling like one of the group. In the end, however, no one trusts the person known as "the office gossip." If you will gossip about one person, everyone knows they can be a target of your gossiping as well. Thus, people may avoid having serious conversations with you, and you may soon find that you're more alienated than you were before you knew anything about anyone.

Power, politics, and hierarchy exist in every organization, group, team, and family, so recognize that the discussion above only points out interactions you have already seen in other areas of your life. Discovery of the power structure in your new workplace is your first mission in your first professional position. You will then be aware of who holds the power and who makes the decisions, and you may operate accordingly, ideally staying above the fray of the office gossip.

ASSIGNMENTS, AND PROJECTS, AND REPORTS—OH, MY!

Especially during your first year, your performance and your work ethic will be under constant scrutiny. Learning exactly what is expected of you will help you make a strong start at your new job. In order to fully understand the organization's expectations, regular and thorough communication with your supervisor and your team members will be essential. As a working professional, you no longer have homework, exams, and papers due. You do, however, have projects, reports, and perhaps accounts, for which you are solely responsible. If you manage your time wisely, you should be effective in getting your duties completed during work hours. As a new employee, though, you may find yourself working harder than others to set yourself apart. It may be helpful for your development as a professional if you take ownership of a few extra things by volunteering for them. This will show your new employer that you take initiative and have ambition. Before getting involved in too many tasks, however, ask yourself if you have the time to complete each one thoroughly. Once your name is attached to a project, its success or failure will be attached to your name. Doing a few things very well is just as good, if not better, than doing several things with mediocrity.

Imagine that you supervise Tom, a new employee who is young, eager, and enthusiastic about his new job. Not only does Tom seem to grasp what is expected of him, he continues to take on new roles and responsibilities on a volunteer basis. As his supervisor, this seems great! It saves you time and effort and allows you to concentrate on other things. Over time, however, you begin to get calls and emails about Tom's projects: things are not getting done, and the things that are getting done are not going well. As a supervisor, the positive image you once had of this young, eager, enthusiastic employee is now replaced by disappointment, and time lost cleaning up messes. Overzealousness can get new employees like Tom into unintended trouble quickly.

Overall, as a new employee it is a strength to show ambition and enthusiasm for a new job by taking on simultaneous responsibilities, but you must first be certain that your primary duties and obligations (including your core training) are complete. Once your work is underway, if you have questions, *ask!* If you mess up, *confess!* You are expected to contribute positively to the organization, but you are not expected to know and do everything; so take initiative, but don't take on more than you can handle.

ETHICAL DILEMMAS

Your success in maintaining a positive professional reputation will depend largely on your own actions. There will be times, though, when you are faced with a problem that is not of your own making. Just because you are on your best be-havior does not mean everyone else is, and once you are a full-time employee, you may be exposed to certain ethical dilemmas. In fact, you may have already been exposed to countless ethical dilemmas in school, part-time jobs, internships, and extracurricular activities. Did you ever see a fellow student cheating on an exam? Or perhaps a fellow part-time employee keeping some extra cash tips without reporting them? Your reactions to those situations will tell you a great deal about how you will react when you face others. Any of your possible actions come with consequences, so you must decide which course to take, based on your own ideas of right and wrong.

Integrity, at its core, is doing the right thing all the time, even when no one is looking. Applying integrity to dilemmas can help to solve them, while maintaining your own self-respect and the respect of your colleagues. As you deal with ethical dilemmas, you must always remember your professional reputation. Again, it is a reputation that will follow you from job to job and career to career, so keeping it respectable is essential. Always remember to maintain your integrity and act ac-cordingly. A few things you should consider as you face such dilemmas:

- Is this behavior legal?

- Is this behavior ethical?

- Is my action/inaction fair to all involved?

- What do my decisions say about me?

- Would I be embarrassed if my actions/inactions were discovered?

- Would authority figures approve?

- What are the consequences (for me, and for others involved)?

If you are not certain what constitutes legal or acceptable behavior in your workplace, do some research, and be sure to use all the resources you have at your disposal. An employee handbook defining formal office policies was likely given to you when you started your new job. Depending upon the size of your organization, you may also have access to legal counsel. And you will always have access to the ear of your mentor, or others in the organization. If all else fails, maintain your integrity, and do the right thing. Refer to Activity 8.1 in the APPENDIX to test your reaction to some ethical dilemmas.

CAUTION: *MULTIPLE GENERATIONS AT WORK*

As with all elements of diversity, generational differences enrich the workplace, but they also provide the potential for challenges. Consider the generations you will be working with in your new position: some may have been born during World War II, some during the counterculture movements of the 1960s, and others during the Internet Revolution of the 1990s. People within each generation tend to have their own preconceived notion about the others. Think about your stereotype of a "baby boomer." What does this person look like in your mind? How do they act? What do they value? While you may have your own image of other generations, they also have preconceived notions about you. Are you viewed as spoiled? Entitled? Technologically savvy? Some of these prejudgments about your generation might be good, but others might be negative. It is important to think about the generations you will work with, and determine how you might be viewed. This may help you to overcome negative stereotypes and better understand expectations related to positive stereotypes.

DIVERSITY IN THE WORKPLACE

One of the greatest aspects of any new experience is getting to meet, observe, and interact with diverse groups of people. Starting a new job will allow you the opportunity to do just that. We all have a unique combination of skills and life experiences; therefore, we are all diverse in the sense that we are all different, and we all look at the world, and our workplace, through a different lens. Awareness of this fact can aid us on the path to building positive, effective, and meaningful interpersonal relationships.

Additionally, organizations seek out this diversity because they recognize that differences are good, and make an organization stronger. One person's strength can compensate for another's weakness. One person's viewpoint takes into account different experiences than another's, and so on. Depending upon your experiences thus far in life, understanding this new group of people might present some challenges.

Think back to your transition from high school to college. As you changed schools or communities, what did you notice about the people around you? Did you have trouble finding your fit within the new surroundings? If you moved from smaller to larger schools—as students often do when going from high school to college—how was the new student population different from your old one? Diversity in the workplace will be a transition for you as well. You and each of your co-workers were chosen by your employer to fill a specific function because of your qualifications and experience. Employers expect that your background will be positive for the organization, and once you have been hired, the diversity of your background will be beneficial in brainstorming ideas and making decisions.

WHAT MAKES US DIVERSE?

- Hometown
- Ethnicity
- Family structure
- Age
- Experiences
- Skill level
- Education
- Personality
- Interests
- Values
- Religion
- Gender
- Sexual orientation
- Socioeconomic status

And so much more!

Conflict is a natural part of human interaction and you will eventually encounter it at work. Many people make a concerted effort to avoid conflict, because it makes them uncomfortable. Indeed, unresolved conflict can lead to the downfall of an organization, but conflict itself can fulfill a vital role in making the organization thrive. Which purpose will it serve in your organization? The answer lies in how conflict is approached. Is it approached with fear and avoidance, or with the intention to resolve it and make the organization stronger? The former approach will allow the conflict to fester, often resulting in personal disappointments, hurt feelings, and decreased morale, all while not solving the issue at hand. The latter approach, however, has the potential to mend relationships, increase productivity, and improve morale.

When you sense conflict arising, confront it early on, in a diplomatic and professional manner. State your observations about behaviors and outcomes (not about the people themselves), and work toward resolution of the conflict. By keeping the focus on the divergence of opinion, and not on the people involved, you stand less chance of unnecessarily offending your co-workers. Some large organizations might have conflict resolution specialists onsite; in other cases, you may have to take the lead in resolution yourself. Consult a mentor or someone in your chain of command for assistance before diving in. However you go about it, remember that temporary discomfort will likely lead to a more effective and productive working environment in the long run.

COMMUNICATION IN THE WORKPLACE

Communication is at the center of all of these interpersonal relationships. Be it written, verbal, or nonverbal, communication is how we send and receive messages, and much of your professional reputation will revolve around this crucial aspect. In fact, sometimes the importance of the message itself is secondary to the delivery. Whenever there are people working together, there will be opportunities for miscommunication. Your goal should be to avoid this wherever possible by planning your approach to communicating with colleagues and clients, and thinking about how others perceive you.

NONVERBAL COMMUNICATION: WHAT YOU'RE SAYING WHEN YOU'RE NOT SAYING ANYTHING

Nonverbal communication is a powerful way to show your attitude, be it good or bad. Imagine you are meeting with your supervisor, presenting the results of a project you have just completed. As you speak, you notice that she is slouching in her chair, arms crossed, with a furrowed brow. This could indicate that she does not like what you're telling the group; or she may just be distracted by something unpleasant that happened before your meeting, and the negative posture may have nothing to do with you. Or perhaps she is deep in thought, carefully processing what you are saying. Either way, you may get the impression that you have done or said something wrong. Think about the messages that you send nonverbally. Imagine yourself in any meeting you have had recently. Consider your posture, facial expression, and other body language. What impression might you be giving? Make a conscious effort to think about this during interactions with colleagues and evaluate yourself accordingly. Make a mental note of how you think you can improve.

Generally speaking, it is good to convey a positive attitude both verbally and nonverbally. Try sitting up straight, making eye contact with people in meetings, and not fidgeting. Even when you disagree with something or someone, there is a positive way to do so. Consider this approach your "professional poker face," which you can use at times when you may need to stifle an immediate reaction to a situation in order to avoid being perceived as too negative, or not a team player.

Beyond body language, another key to nonverbal communication of who you are is your dress. How do you measure up to your colleagues? If you hope to eventually be promoted within your organization, take note of how your superiors dress. It is often said that in order to move on, you should dress not for the job you have, but for the job you want. A professional appearance can be just as important as any other aspect of communication. As with all things discussed in this chapter, if you are not sure how you should dress, ask! The employee handbook may include guidance, and asking (and observing) your supervisor or your new colleagues will likely get you a quick, reliable answer as well.

VERBAL COMMUNICATION: WHICH MESSAGES DO YOU COMMUNICATE AND HOW?

While nonverbal cues are a major part of your communication (helping it, or perhaps hindering it), the way you speak is also of great importance. Right or wrong, people are often judged initially based on how they speak. Your overall speech patterns are likely well-formed at this point, but there is always room for improvement. During your interview, you were probably especially careful about what you said and how you said it. Now that you have the job, it might be tempting to let that mentality go, because it takes much effort. In reality, remember that this will likely not be your last job. You are in a nearly constant state of interviewing, be it for promotional consideration, or a change of job entirely. That said, you must always consider your grammatical correctness, and your overall patterns of verbal communications such as when you speak, how much you speak, and the professional nature of your language.

Be aware of how meetings and informal interactions are conducted. Talking more than anyone else, especially at first, can leave the impression that you are arrogant and that you tend to jump to conclusions before being fully informed and aware of the situation. On the other hand, talking less than anyone else can lead to the impression that you lack confidence and/or knowledge. Be aware of when it is appropriate for you to offer your input in meetings and brainstorming sessions. You'll earn trust and credibility over time, but in the meantime, you may wish to watch others' reactions to help you decide when to contribute aloud. Remember too, that you were hired for a reason. If they did not care about what you have to offer, you would still be interviewing for positions.

Using slang, and especially profanity, in your work setting should be done only with great caution, if at all. Even if others speak this way, you may leave a negative impression if you conform to this pattern while you are new. Remember, you are joining a group of people who know each other fairly well and you are still an unknown to them. Make a good impression by speaking with correct grammar, little slang, and no profanity, until you are no longer new (usually one year on the job). In a broader sense, consider your tone. Are you conveying the message that you are open to feedback, or is your spoken communication closed and final? Whether or not you are open to alternatives will be obvious in the openness of your communication and, rest assured, when you are new, others will be watching for these clues.

WHAT IS YOUR VERBAL COMMUNICATION STYLE?

As you may remember from CHAPTER 1, psychiatrist Carl Jung theorized that we all have a unique personality that drives many of our behaviors; certain human behaviors that may seem random to the untrained eye are actually quite orderly and structured, based on elements of our innate personality preferences. Among other differences, some of us are extraverted (drawing energy from the outside world), and some of us are introverted (drawing energy from our own inner world).

People with an extraverted preference tend to process information out loud and thus, may seem to talk a lot.

People with an introverted preference tend to process information internally and thus, may appear shy, slow, or altogether removed from a discussion.

Which is your preference? How does it show itself in your daily communications? Are you as tolerant of others' personality preferences as you hope they are of yours?

WRITTEN COMMUNICATION: IT'S AN E-WORLD, WE ONLY TYPE IN IT

Much of your communication in the workplace will not involve a face-to-face exchange of words, nor will it offer you the benefit of nonverbal feedback. Much of it will instead be typed in email messages, without the benefit of your delivery or seeing the other person's reaction, or reacting to others in real time. This might have its benefits for you, but it will certainly have its challenges as well. Have you ever been speaking with someone and you quickly realize via their nonverbal communication that they are terribly confused or perhaps unnecessarily offended by what you are saying? In these situations, you have the opportunity to quickly correct course and diffuse the situation. Written communication does not offer that luxury and thus, you must be careful, precise, and concise in your written communication.

Most of your written communication until this point has likely been via informal email with friends and family, or even the more informal method of text messaging, or messaging friends on social networking sites. In these communications, it is common and accepted to use slang, abbreviations, and creative acronyms. Think back to the discussion of generational differences in the workplace. Does

WHAT IS THE MESSAGE OF THIS EMAIL?

Sue,

Thanks for giving me that report yesterday.

John

On the surface, it looks simple, but even the simplest of messages can be misinterpreted. What is John really trying to say here?

Thanks for giving me that report yesterday.
Thanks for giving *me* that report yesterday.
Thanks for giving me *that* report yesterday.
Thanks for giving me that report *yesterday.*

It could be any of these, depending upon where John placed his emphasis. Without actually hearing him say this sentence, Sue may be at a loss for where to go next due to her confusion over the ambiguous phrasing. Or, perhaps even worse, she could take action based on her perception of what he meant, rather than his actual meaning. Given all of the possible meanings, if the written message is at all unclear, be careful with how you respond. Never send a reactionary response when you are angry, upset, or uncertain about what is being communicated. Get clarification, ask questions, and pick up the phone or set up an appointment with the sender to discuss his/her intent.

your grandpa know what ROTFL means? Perhaps not. Your baby boomer boss or co-workers may not, either. In business communications, lose the slang and acronyms and write in complete, grammatically correct sentences (with upper-case letters at the beginning of sentences and a punctuation mark at the end), so as to leave no room for error in your communications.

In addition to the way you compose a professional email, consider your message. A good rule of thumb is to never send any email that you would be embarrassed to read on a billboard. Eventually, sometime, somewhere, someone will accidentally click "reply to all" instead of "reply" and everyone will read what you wrote. Or, the recipient may print the message, keep it in their inbox for months, or worse, accidentally forward it along to someone else. Email is not a "safe" form of communication, and in the workplace it should be reserved for professional correspondence only.

Sarcasm always comes across well in writing. Did you catch that joke? Perhaps you read that without the benefit of the author's inflection on "always." If so, you just witnessed a miscommunication in writing due to sarcasm. Sarcasm and hyperbole very rarely translate in writing, because so much of both depend on the tone and verbal delivery. Due to the possibility for extra problems in communicating with others, avoid sarcasm in your written correspondence. In fact, many people frown on sarcasm altogether because of the extra effort involved in deciphering it, as well as the opportunity for miscommunication.

In all forms of workplace written communication, you should strive for the transfer of important information in a concise and well-written manner. Be brief, clear, and complete in your written communication. This shows respect for others' time, and conveys the heart of your message without being too verbose. Shorter emails, memos, and letters are more likely to be read, and thus, more likely to be responded to.

YOUR LONG-TERM SUCCESS

This review of transitions has largely been in reference to your first year or so on the job. During this time, though, it is crucial for you to be thinking about your long-term success. Where will you be in five to ten years, and how will you get there? Earlier in this text, we reviewed methods for networking to help you locate open positions; do not neglect the importance of networking for your long-term success. As stated many times in this text, this first job will likely not be your last job. That said, you must begin thinking about your future the moment you set foot in the door of your new position. With the assistance of mentors and the benefit of professional development, you will continue to increase your marketability in the workforce, be it for possible promotions within your current organization, or for a future move into a new one.

MENTORS

Becoming an effective and influential professional will take time and patience, and you may benefit greatly from the advice and input of a mentor. Some organizations recognize the positive impact of mentors and have formalized mentoring programs. Take advantage of this resource if it is available to you. If there is no formal structure, you can create your own. Be on the lookout for influential members of the organization, or elsewhere. Whom do you respect? Who is respected by others? Whose behavior do you wish to emulate? These questions can assist you in choosing a mentor who will aid your long-term quest for success. Since many of the discussions you will have with your mentor may revolve around your chain of command, office politics, ethical dilemmas, or problems with your work, it is usually best to choose a mentor who is somewhat removed from these arenas. If your mentor is receptive, try setting up a formal meeting to check in: perhaps lunch once a month, depending of course upon his/her availability. This will allow you to meet with your mentor in good times and in bad, not just when a problem arises and you need assistance.

KEEPING UP WITH THE TIMES: PROFESSIONAL DEVELOPMENT

Though you have recently completed a formal educational program, you will only be cutting edge for a short time, unless you make a concerted effort to remain in the know about new developments in your industry. For this reason, it is essential to your long-term success to remain educated via publications, conferences, training, networking events, and continuing education. Your employer may recognize the importance of this for your contributions to the organization and thus, may encourage your participation. Other employers will be less enthusiastic about spending money on your professional development. In this case, you may have more success in securing professional development funds after you have been with the organization for awhile, and perhaps more important, after you have proven you are worthy of continued investment. Whether the organization is paying or not, it is your responsibility to remain educated, so join professional organizations, and fund your own professional development if you must.

CONCLUSION

As you embark on the exciting journey that is your professional life, remember to enjoy it. You will meet new people, accomplish great things, and find satisfaction in your newfound independence. Mistakes and missteps may well be a part of this journey. Just like all mistakes in life, however, these can serve you well in the long run as you consider ways to improve your behaviors and make efforts to minimize repeat incidents. Take advantage of opportunities as they arise, and do not underestimate your ability to contribute positively to your new organization. Your professional reputation, relationship management, communication style, and decision-making ability will all develop over time. Patience and persistence will be of great importance as you navigate your way through the world of work. Let your integrity be your guide, and do not hesitate to rely on others when the need arises. Most of all, enjoy the journey, and make the most of your accumulated life experiences by making a positive contribution to the professional world!

CHAPTER SUMMARY AND KEY POINTS:

- Interpersonal relationships are at the core of your professional reputation and can help or hinder your ability to succeed.

- Challenges and ethical dilemmas will arise, and are best handled by maintaining your integrity and reaching a fair conclusion.

- Independence and completing work tasks are essential, and new employees should avoid taking on too much.

- Verbal, nonverbal, and written communication are all essential to forming and maintaining relationships, as well as accomplishing tasks and furthering your career.

- Your long-term success will be more likely if you rely on mentors and continue to stay apprised of new developments in your field.

REFERENCES

Brown, D. (1995). A values-based approach to facilitating career transitions. Career Development Quarterly, 44(1), 4–11.

Browse by O*NET Descriptor. (n.d.). In O*NET OnLine. Retrieved from http://online.onetcenter.org/find/descriptor/browse/Work_Activities/.

Bureau of Labor Statistics (2007). Retrieved January 22, 2009, at http://www.bls.gov/oco/oco20042.htm.

Corey, G. (2005). Theory and practice of counseling and psychotherapy. Belmont, CA: Thomson Learning, Inc.

Figler, H. (1999). The complete job-search handbook (3rd ed.). New York, NY: Henry Holt and Company, LLC.

Goodman, P. (2001). Win-win career negotiations. Washington, DC: Gut Instinct Press.

Gottfredson, G. D., & Holland, J. L. (1996). Dictionary of Holland occupational codes (3rd ed.). Odessa, FL: Psychological Assessment Resources, Inc.

Grutter, J., & Hammer, A. (2005). Strong interest inventory user's guide. Mountain View, CA: CPP, Inc.

Hoefflin, N. (Ed.). (1998). Choices & challenges: Job search strategies for liberal arts students (3rd ed.). Bloomington, IN: Indiana University Custom Publishing and Indiana University Career Development Center.

Lakhani, D. (2005). Persuasion. Hoboken, NJ: John Wiley & Sons, Inc.

Mariani, M. (2003). Job search in the age of Internet. Occupational Outlook Quarterly, Bureau of Labor Statistics, 8–9.

Myers, I. (1998). Introduction to type (6th ed.). Mountain View, CA: CPP, Inc.

NACE Web Job Outlook Surveys (2006–2008). Retrieved from http://www.naceweb.org/pubs/JobOutlook/2007/default.htm.

OECD Economic Outlook (2002). Retrieved from http://findarticles.com/p/articles/mi_m4456/is_2002_Dec/ai_98032790.

Skills search. (n.d.). In O*NET OnLine. Retrieved from http://online.onetcenter.org/skills/#group1.

Tyson, E. (2006). Personal finance for dummies (5th ed.). Hoboken, NJ: Wiley Publishing, Inc.

ACTIVITIES

CHAPTER ONE

ACTIVITY 1.1: DISCOVER BELIEFS ABOUT YOURSELF AND WORK

This activity will help you become aware of beliefs you have about yourself and work. Write down as many beliefs as you can, positive and/or negative, by responding to the following:

- What do I believe about work generally, and/or the specific job or career I'm interested in? (example: "Work is something you have to do, not something you want to do.")
- What do I believe about my own abilities to succeed in the job search? (example: "My internship experience will help me get a great job.")

If you're having trouble articulating your beliefs, think about your recent job search behaviors (or lack thereof). What beliefs might underlie your actions or inaction?

You can also try finishing sentences that begin with these words and phrases:

"I believe that work…"
"I believe that my career choice…"
"I believe that my job search…"

Think each phrase to yourself silently and wait, allowing your beliefs to present themselves when they're ready.

ACTIVITY 1.2: DISCOVER BELIEFS ABOUT YOUR GOALS

This activity will help you discover beliefs that may help or hinder you as you work toward a goal. First, write a specific career goal that you currently have (example: "Obtain a theatre internship in New York City for next summer"). Next, write down positive and negative beliefs that you have about achieving this specific goal:

- Positive beliefs (example: "If I expand my network in New York City, I will definitely land a cool internship.")
- Negative or limiting beliefs (example: "Living in New York City is too expensive.")

ACTIVITY 1.3: DISCOVER BELIEFS ABOUT YOUR CAREER DEVELOPMENT

This activity will help you discover positive and negative beliefs you may hold about your career development generally. Write about your short-term and long-term career plans and goals. Let your thoughts flow freely without judging or critiquing what you write. Next, reread what you wrote. Look for beliefs that may be either obvious or subtly implied. Write them down.

ACTIVITY 1.4: WRITE YOUR EPITAPH

Imagine that it's many years from now. You've lived a satisfying life that was full and complete. Write your own epitaph or obituary. What would you say about your life, especially about your work life? What made your work so satisfying?

Mark each of the 35 work values below as L, M or H (L=low or no importance to me, M=medium importance to me, H=high importance to me):

_____ *Advancement:* there are ample promotional opportunities in my organization or career field

_____ *Benefits:* my employer offers benefits such as vacation and sick leave, health and life insurance plans, and retirement plans

_____ *Challenge:* my work challenges me

_____ *Colleagues:* my supervisor and coworkers are supportive and friendly

_____ *Competition:* my workplace is a competitive environment

_____ *Creativity:* I have opportunities to express my creativity

_____ *Ethics:* I respect my employer and do not experience situations that could conflict with my ethical standards

_____ *Flexibility (scheduling hours):* I have flexibility in setting my schedule of work hours

_____ *Flexibility (while working):* I have flexibility in planning my time while at work

_____ *Goals and Results:* my work is goal-oriented and I see the results of my efforts

_____ *Independence:* I have autonomy in my work tasks and am minimally supervised

_____ *Interest:* my work is interesting to me and a very important part of my life

_____ *Leadership:* my work offers leadership opportunities

_____ *Learning (High):* my work requires ongoing learning

_____ *Learning (Low):* after initial training, my work requires little learning

_____ *Location:* my workplace is close to my home and commuting time is minimal

_____ *Management:* my work provides opportunities to supervise and manage others

_____ *Moral Fulfillment:* my work contributes to my higher ideals

_____ *Pay and Profit:* I am well compensated for my work

_____ *People:* my work involves significant people contact

_____ *Power:* I have power and authority in making decisions and setting policy

_____ *Pressure and Pace (High):* the pressure and pace of my work is high

_____ *Pressure and Pace (Low):* the pressure and pace of my work is low

_____ *Prestige:* my title and/or work is prestigious and commands respect and attention

_____ *Recognition:* I receive positive feedback for a job well done

_____ *Security:* my job security is high

_____ *Supervision:* I receive high quality supervision

_____ *Teamwork (High):* much of my work is done on teams

_____ *Teamwork (Low):* my job requires little, if any, teamwork

_____ *Training:* the training program is excellent and thorough

_____ *Travel (High):* I travel extensively

_____ *Travel (Low):* I rarely travel or do not travel

_____ *Variety:* my work offers variety in tasks

_____ *Workspace:* I have a private workspace or office

_____ *Work/Life Balance:* I feel comfortable with the balance between my work life and personal life

Finally, create a list of your top work values by writing down all the values you marked H. If you've thought of values that aren't on the above list, feel free to add them to the list.

Read the brief descriptions of the Holland interest themes below. Then rank the themes 1 to 6 in accordance with your interests (1=high, 6=low):

Rank	Interest Theme
	Realistic (Doers): These people enjoy mechanical/construction activities, using tools. See self as practical, having mechanical skills. Like nature and outdoor environments. Career motivator: using physical skill.
	Investigative (Thinkers): These people enjoy exploring new facts or theories, prediction or control of natural and social phenomena. See self as intelligent and skeptical. Like academic/research environments. Career motivator: analyzing.
	Artistic (Creators): These people enjoy creative and expressive activities including literary, musical, or artistic activities. See self as open to experience, innovative. Career motivator: expressing creativity.
	Social (Helpers): These people enjoy helping, teaching, treating, counseling, or serving others through personal interaction. See self as empathetic, patient, and having interpersonal skills. Career motivator: helping others.
	Enterprising (Persuaders): These people enjoy persuading and directing others toward organizational goals and economic success. See self as having sales and persuasive ability. Career motivator: persuading and influencing.
	Conventional (Organizers): These people enjoy data management tasks and activities that require organization, detail, and accuracy. See self as having technical skills in business or production. Career motivator: organizing.

To further explore and precisely articulate your interest themes, and to discover how your interests relate to specific occupations, ask your career center if they offer assessments such as the Strong Interest Inventory or Self-Directed Search.

ACTIVITY 1.7: CREATE YOUR DREAM JOB

Write about your dream job, the job that you think would totally satisfy you. If you've never considered this, take some time to fantasize about what your ideal job might be like. This job may or may not exist in the "real world," but even if it doesn't, you could be the first to do it—after all, new kinds of work are created every day! Consider the following questions: In your dream job, what do you do all day long? What is it about this job that is so satisfying? Why does doing this work bring more satisfaction than doing nothing at all? Alternatively, consider what you would do if you won millions in the lottery. After a few years of relaxing, you might start to get bored. What work would you do if you didn't need to earn money?

ACTIVITY 1.8: BRAINSTORM YOUR INTERESTS

Make a list of every interest you currently have, have had recently, and have been thinking about exploring in the near future. Your interests might be related to paid or volunteer work, sports and hobbies, TV shows and movies, books and newspapers, classes and other learning activities, student organizations, and activities with friends and family. After you've completed your list, look for patterns and themes among your interests. What do you see?

ACTIVITY 1.9: ASSESS YOUR PERSONAL ATTRIBUTES

Check off which "personal attributes" you possess or that describe you, and write notes about those you'd like to develop or improve. Some attributes may be more, or less, relevant in specific work environments.

Describes Me	Attribute	Notes
	Accurate	
	Compassionate	
	Creative	
	Decisive	
	Dedicated / Committed	
	Determined	
	Diplomatic	
	Empathetic	
	Encouraging / Supportive	
	Energetic	
	Enthusiastic	
	Ethical	
	Fair	
	Flexible / Adaptable	
	Friendly / Personable	
	Generous	
	Honest	
	Integrity	
	Mindful	
	Motivated	
	Open-minded	
	Organized	
	Outgoing	
	Patient	
	Polite	
	Positive	
	Professional / Businesslike	
	Punctual	
	Quiet	
	Respectful of diversity	
	Responsible / Reliable	
	A risk taker	
	Self-confident	
	Self-disciplined	
	Sense of humor	
	Service oriented	
	Strong work ethic	
	Task-focused	
	Warm	
	Willing to learn	

ACTIVITY 1.10: DEFINE YOUR EMPLOYABLE SKILLS

Define your employable skills by placing a checkmark in the box next to each skill that you have used in any work or academic setting. Think carefully before concluding that you have never used a skill. Then, review the checked skills and circle those that are most developed and that you would enjoy using on the job. Refer to this exercise when writing your resume and cover letter.

☐ **Administer**
Perform day-to-day tasks such as maintaining information files and processing paperwork.

☐ **Advise / Counsel / Consult**
Provide guidance, support, or expert advice to individuals or groups.

☐ **Analyze**
Identify the underlying principles, reasons, or facts by breaking down information or data into separate parts.

☐ **Appraise / Assess**
Estimate or evaluate the value, importance, or quality of an object or real estate.

☐ **Assemble**
Put or piece together parts of an object or information.

☐ **Assist / Treat**
Provide personal assistance, medical attention, emotional support, or other care to others such as coworkers, customers, or patients.

☐ **Budget**
Determine how money will be spent to get the work done, and account for these expenditures.

☐ **Build a team**
Encourage and build mutual trust, respect, and cooperation among team members.

☐ **Build relationships**
Develop constructive and cooperative working relationships with others, and maintain them over time.

☐ **Calculate**
Use mathematics to solve problems.

☐ **Canvass**
Go through a region to solicit votes, subscriptions, or orders; conduct a survey of public opinion.

☐ **Coach / Mentor**
Serve as a trusted counselor, teacher, or guide by identifying the developmental needs of others and helping them to improve their knowledge or skills.

☐ **Collaborate**
Work together with others on a common project.

☐ **Collect**
Call and obtain payment for monies due; take in donations.

☐ **Communicate**
Provide information to supervisors, coworkers, or subordinates.

☐ **Conceive**
Form or develop an idea in the mind.

☐ **Construct**
Make or form by putting together materials and parts; create by organizing ideas or arguments.

☐ **Coordinate**
Adjust actions in relation to others' actions.

☐ **Coordinate a team**
Get members of a group to work together to accomplish tasks.

☐ **Correspond**
Communicate with others in writing.

☐ **Create**
Develop new ideas, systems, or products.

☐ **Decide**
Analyze information, consider the relative costs and benefits of potential actions, and choose the most appropriate action.

☐ **Design**
Plan and fashion the form and structure of an object, work of art, or decorative scheme.

☐ **Dispense / Distribute**
Pass out, ship, or deliver information or goods to individuals or retailers.

☐ **Display**
Spread out merchandise for viewing by the public; present objects for a public exhibition.

☐ **Draft / Lay out / Specify**
Provide documentation, detailed instructions, drawings, or specifications to tell others about how devices, parts, equipment, or structures are to be constructed, assembled, maintained, or used.

☐ **Edit**
Direct the preparation of a publication; revise or correct a manuscript; assemble components of a video or audio presentation by deleting, arranging, or splicing.

☐ **Entertain / Perform**
Show hospitality or engage the attention of others.

☐ **Estimate**
Make an approximate judgment of sizes, distances, and quantities; determine time, costs, resources, or materials needed to perform a work activity.

☐ **Facilitate**
Assist and support a group of people to function effectively toward the achievement of an outcome.

☐ **Inspect**
Inspect equipment, structures, or materials to identify the cause of errors or other problems or defects.

☐ **Install**
Install equipment, machines, wiring, or programs to meet specifications.

☐ **Interpret / Explain**
Translate or explain what information means and how it can be used, in terms that can be easily understood.

☐ **Learn**
Assimilate new knowledge or skill for both current and future problem-solving and decision-making.

☐ **Listen**
Give full attention to what other people are saying, taking time to understand the points being made, asking questions as appropriate, and not interrupting at inappropriate times.

☐ **Maintain**
Perform routine maintenance on equipment and determine when and what kind of maintenance is needed.

☐ **Manage materials**
Obtain and see to the appropriate use of equipment, facilities, and materials needed to do certain work.

☐ **Manage time**
Manage one's own time and the time of others.

☐ **Measure**
Ascertain dimensions, quantity, or capacity by comparison with a standard.

☐ **Mediate / Handle complaints**
Resolve and settle grievances, conflicts, and complaints.

☐ **Monitor**
Monitor and assess the performance of yourself, others, organizations, machines, or the environment to detect or assess problems, make improvements, or take corrective action.

☐ **Motivate**
Provide guidance and encouragement to others.

☐ **Move / Handle**
Use hands and arms in handling, positioning, and moving materials.

☐ **Negotiate**
Bring others together and attempt to reconcile differences.

☐ **Observe**
Observe, receive, and otherwise obtain information from all relevant sources.

☐ **Operate**
Control operations of equipment or systems.

☐ **Organize / Plan**
Develop specific goals and plans to prioritize, organize, and accomplish your work.

☐ **Perform physical activity**
Perform physical activities that require considerable use of your arms and legs and moving your whole body, such as climbing, lifting, balancing, walking, stooping, and handling of materials.

☐ **Persuade**
Persuade others to change their minds or behavior.

☐ **Present**
Show or offer something to an audience.

☐ **Process / Audit**
Compile, categorize, calculate, audit, or verify information or data.

☐ **Program**
Write computer programs for various purposes.

☐ **Project / Predict**
Calculate, estimate, or forecast a future situation or event based on present data or trends.

☐ **Promote / Publicize**
Encourage the sales or acceptance of a product or service through advertising or by notifying the public, contribute to the growth of an organization or cause.

☐ **Protect**
Defend or guard a person, place, or object from loss, injury, or danger.

☐ **Recruit / Interview**
Recruit, interview, select, and hire employees.

☐ **Repair**
Repair electronic and/or mechanical devices or systems using the needed tools.

☐ **Represent**
Act for or on behalf of a person, group, or organization.

☐ **Research**
Search for facts or information in a systematic manner.

☐ **Review**
Write a critique of a book, drama, or musical performance.

☐ **Schedule**
Schedule events, programs, and activities, as well as the work of others.

☐ **Select equipment**
Determine the kind of tools and/or equipment needed to do a job.

☐ **Select learning strategies**
Select and use training/instructional methods and procedures appropriate for the situation when learning or teaching.

☐ **Sell**
Convince others to buy merchandise/goods or to otherwise change their minds or actions.

☐ **Serve**
Serve customers in restaurants and stores, and receive clients or guests.

☐ **Set up**
Prepare a physical space for a particular purpose or event.

☐ **Sketch**
Represent, describe, or portray roughly or briefly.

☐ **Solve problems**
Identify problems and review relevant information to develop and evaluate options and implement solutions.

☐ **Speak (in public)**
Talk to small and large groups to convey information effectively.

☐ **Strategize**
Establish long-range objectives and specify the actions to achieve them.

☐ **Supervise / Manage**
Motivate, develop, and direct people as they work.

☐ **Teach / Instruct**
Identify educational needs of others, develop educational or training programs or classes, and teach or instruct them.

☐ **Think critically**
Use logic and reasoning to identify the strengths and weaknesses of alternative solutions, conclusions, or approaches to problems.

☐ **Transcribe / Record**
Enter, transcribe, record, or maintain information in written or electronic form.

☐ **Translate**
Restate words from one language into another.

☐ **Troubleshoot**
Determine causes of errors and decide what to do about them.

☐ **Understand written information**
Understand written work-related documents.

☐ **Update**
Keep up-to-date technically and apply new knowledge to your job.

☐ **Write**
Communicate effectively in writing as appropriate for the needs of the audience.

ACTIVITY 1.11: ARTICULATE YOUR TOP SKILLS

Now that you've identified your skills, choose three that are likely to be relevant to your next job or internship. For each skill, describe how you developed it, and how applying that skill has contributed to an organization, project, or employer. Doing this exercise will show you how to think about and articulate your skills on a resume, in a cover letter, or in an interview.

Example:

Skill:	Teach
How Developed:	*Taught multiple yoga classes at an after-school program for over 70 high school juniors and seniors.*
Resulting Contributions:	*Had many students return to subsequent classes; many students reported feeling more in shape and centered during school activities. Student evaluations were very high. As a result of this experience, my college recreational sports center asked me to teach non-credit yoga classes for my peers.*

CHAPTER THREE

ACTIVITY 3.1: IDENTIFY YOUR CURRENT NETWORK

On a separate sheet of paper, brainstorm a list of names of all the people you currently know. Include friends, family, neighbors, doctors, professors, advisors, former employers; in short, everyone you know.

Name & Contact Information	Connection	Notable Point
Max Doe City of Indianapolis 317.578.1793 jdoe@gmail.com	Friend of Sister	Works in training and development; met at holiday party.

ACTIVITY 3.2: CRAFT YOUR MESSAGE

On a separate sheet of paper, write an overview of your experiences as a student, your upcoming plans, and specify the type of information or contacts you are requesting.

ACTIVITY 3.3: ORGANIZE YOUR JOB SEARCH AND TAKE ACTION

Document each strategy and record relevant contact information, results, and next steps. Update your Job Search Action List regularly! (Use the following table as a template to create your own table or spreadsheet; remember to focus your search on the hidden job market.)

Job Search Action List

Strategy	Specific Name	Contacts	Date/Outcome	Next Steps
Alumni Association	Indiana University	Jane Henry Director of Alumni Relations jdoe@indiana.edu	Oct 5: Given directions on use of online directory and upcoming chapter events	Find and contact 3 alumni in Training & Development
Professional Associations	ASTD: American Society for Training and Development	Lisa Miller Member Services lmiller@astd.org www.astd.org	Oct 5: Found local chapter website and chose upcoming event. http://www.ciastd.org/	Attend networking lunch on Oct. 11
	SHRM: Society for Human Resource Management	www.shrm.org	Oct 7: Found local events	Attend workshop on Oct. 20
Networking Groups	Young Professionals of City	Sally Mae President same@YPC.org	Oct 6: Spoke with Sally; found out about YPC's mission and events	Attend Oct. event (last Tues. of each month)

Other sections of your job search action list might include employment agencies, informational interviews, school's career center, targeted employers, and the Chamber of Commerce.

CHAPTER FOUR

ACTIVITY 4.1: GATHER YOUR RAW MATERIAL INTO AN "EVERYTHING" DOCUMENT

- Write down each group you've belonged to since high school, devoting a whole blank side of a sheet of paper to each group. This includes sports teams, clubs, sororities, fraternities, outreach groups, volunteer organizations, and employers.
- For each group, write down the roles you filled (for example, "member," "captain," "treasurer") or titles of positions you held.
- Now write down every task that you did in each role, what method you used to do it, why it was worth doing, and the result of your doing it.

When it comes time to craft a resume for a specific job or internship, you can draw from this raw material. Of course, you will still want to craft each accomplishment statement by using the words of the employer when possible. For example, if you wrote that you "Oversaw" teammates, but the job or internship posting wants you to have "Supervised" others, use the employer's language.

ACTIVITY 4.2: LINKING WHAT YOU'VE DONE TO THE EMPLOYER'S NEEDS

Every time you apply for a job or internship, you must find a way to relate what you've done in the past to what the employer needs done now. Practice this now using a relatively detailed job or internship ad.

Part One: *Profiling the Employer*

Read the job or internship ad and answer these questions about the open position on a separate sheet of paper.

- What is the organization name and position title?

- List 4–5 major responsibilities of the position (be specific—what will you be expected to accomplish on a weekly basis?)
- List 7–10 required skills or knowledge (be as specific as possible)
- List any unwritten demands you can expect (think about it—what can you infer?)

Part Two: *What You Offer*

Using your "everything" document, pick one group or organization that you've been part of and try to match what you did there to what the employer wants. This will become a customized experience block.

- List the name of the old organization and your title there
- List 4–5 responsibilities from the old position
- List 7–10 required skills or knowledge used in the old position
- List 3–4 achievements and contributions you made to the old organization

Part Three: *Tying It Together*

Now match it up. Make two columns and write out the employer's needs from part one in the left column, then match each need with something you did at your old job. Try to do this for as many responsibilities or skills and knowledge listed in part one as possible. An example is given below.

Employer's Needs	Your Experience
A candidate with the ability to sell ideas or products to a wide variety of clients and customers.	Effectively marketed university student services as an admissions tour guide: hosted over 30 groups of students and families from all over the country and from a variety of backgrounds.

ACTIVITY 4.3: RESUME SELF-REVIEW

Go through the following checklist to review your resume before anyone else does.

1. More impressive experience blocks should appear nearer the top than less impressive experience blocks. Does your resume do this? If not, how could you categorize your experiences differently?

2. More important information in a line should appear to the left of less important information (e.g., your job title should be to the left of the dates that you worked there). Does your resume do this? If not, how can you reorganize it?

3. Does your resume show that you will have (on graduation) the required degree, certification, and knowledge required by the job or internship ad? If not, what's missing?

4. Do your category titles (e.g., "Experience") have anything specifically to do with the ad?

5. Do the resume bullets relate at all to the ad? Put a check next to the ones that do and an X next to the ones that don't.

6. Are any memberships listed without description? Decide whether these should be cut or expanded, and write "cut" or "expand" next to them on your resume.

7. Does your resume list any unnecessary information in the Education section (like high school)? If so, cross it out.

8. Is the contact information clearly described and professional?

9. If two addresses are given, are dates also provided so the reader can tell when to use each address?

10. How are the layout and formatting? If you want to change something but don't know how, write down what bothers you and see a career advisor about it.

CHAPTER SIX

ACTIVITY 6.1: PREPARING FOR THE INTERVIEW

This activity is designed to help you prepare for the interview by comparing the skills and knowledge sought by the employer to your own experience. By identifying specific examples of your knowledge and skills, you will be better equipped to speak about your experience and qualifications in a meaningful way during an interview.

Refer to the job description (or one that is similar) of the job you will be interviewing for. Identify 8–10 of the following from the job description and record them:

- Transferable skills

- Specialized knowledge

Refer to your resume. For each transferable skill and piece of specialized knowledge you indentified above, list the following:

- The transferable skill or specialized knowledge

- An experience (part-time or full-time job; or internship, volunteer, classroom, or extracurricular experience) where the skill was used (try to draw upon a variety of experiences); give the specific name of the organization or class

- A brief description of a specific instance when the skill was used

ACTIVITY 6.2: INTERVIEW QUESTIONS

Below are interview questions organized by category. Based on the numbers given in parentheses for each question type, choose questions you would like to practice answering and then:

1. On a sheet of paper, type out each question you selected.

2. Outline an answer underneath each question, making sure you follow the rules given in the chapter, including using SPAR (tell a story).

3. Using your notes as a guide, practice improvising an answer as if you were in an interview. Alternatively, you might ask a friend to ask you the questions and give you feedback on your responses.

I. **General questions (choose 4 from the list below):**

- Tell me about yourself.
- Why did you major in _____?
- What are your strengths?
- What are your weaknesses?
- Where do you hope to be in three years? Five years?
- Why should I hire you over other candidates?
- What kind of supervisor do you prefer?
- How do you handle stress?
- What do you know about our organization?
- Why do you want this job?

II. **Behavior-based questions (choose 4 from the list below):**

- Tell me about a time when you had a conflict with a coworker or customer and how you resolved it.
- Tell me about a time when you accepted constructive feedback from a coworker or supervisor.

- Give me a specific example of a time in which you had to conform to a policy with which you did not agree.

- Tell me about a time when you were able to use your persuasion skills to influence someone's opinion.

- Give an example of a time when you worked as part of a team to complete a project.

- Give an example of a time when you used good judgment in solving a problem.

- Tell me about a time when you showed initiative and took the lead.

- Tell me about a time you were required to be inventive or creative.

- Tell me about a time when you got results at school against all odds. How did you accomplish that and what were the results?

- Give me an example of a time when you broke down a process to make recommendations for improvement.

III.   Stress or testing questions (choose 1 from the list below, if applicable):

- Why were you not more involved during college?

- Why is your GPA so low?

- Why is there a large gap in your work experience?

IV.   Off-the-wall questions (choose 1 from the list below):

- Which song best describes your personality? Why?

- What is the most recent book you read?

- How do you incorporate fun into the workplace?

- How many dogs are there in the United States?

- Who do you admire most and why?

This activity is designed to assist you in reflecting about your interview perfor-mance, be it a real one or practice.

Create a table with 3 columns and 14 rows. Do the following:

1. In the first row, label each column as follows:
    - Interview component
    - Strength
    - Weakness

2. Label each of the 13 remaining rows under "Interview component" column with the following:
    - Preparation
    - Questions I asked
    - Verbal communication
    - Nonverbal communication
    - Nerves management
    - Examining intent (rule 1)
    - Story telling (rule 2)
    - Relevance (rule 3)
    - Positive attitude (rule 4)
    - Attire
    - Other (anything not covered above)
    - The organization (your thoughts on potentially working for the organization)
    - The position (your thoughts on potentially having that job)

3. Now, think back to your interview (or review the recording of your practice interview if you recorded it). For each component listed in the first column, describe what you did well in the interview under the "strength" column and what you could improve under "weakness." (You might have some components that were both a strength and weakness.)

4. Once you have written something about each component, review your analysis. Use it in preparation for your next interview—celebrating and gaining confidence about what you do well and improving upon your weaknesses. Should you advance further in your candidacy for a particular position, review your notes concerning your thoughts about the organization to help you make a decision or to prepare questions for the next round.

CHAPTER SEVEN

ACTIVITY 7.1: ESTABLISH A BUDGET

Using the example on p. 129 as a guide, create your own monthly budget using spreadsheet software such as Microsoft Excel. Add or delete categories as necessary for your personal situation. If you'll be moving somewhere else, make sure to factor in the cost of living in your new location. Use spreadsheet formulas so that each expense you enter is subtracted from your beginning net monthly income. Keep changing amounts until your planned expenses, savings, and debt repayment exactly equal your net monthly income.

ACTIVITY 7.2: COMPARE YOUR VALUES AND GOALS TO A JOB OFFER

This activity will allow you to consider your values and goals and compare them to a job offer (or if you do not yet have an offer, an optimal offer). Make four columns on a sheet of lined paper. In the first column, list the following items:

- Salary
- Starting Date
- Moving Expenses
- Vacation
- Early Reviews
- Flex Time
- Workspace
- Performance Bonuses
- Geographic Location
- Office Space
- Parking

- Housing Allowance
- Travel Allowance
- Stock Options
- Company Car
- Retention Bonuses
- College Tuition Reimbursement

At the top of the second column, write "Offer meets needs or item unimportant." At the top of the third column, write "I minimally need." At the top of the fourth, write "I optimally want."

Then, go through the list one by one. Mark a check in the second column if the offer meets your needs for that item, or if that item is not important to you. If you would like to negotiate that item, write what you minimally need in the third column, and/or what you optimally want in the fourth column.

CHAPTER EIGHT

ACTIVITY 8.1: RESPONDING TO ETHICAL DILEMMAS

Read the ethical dilemmas below, and think about how you would react. What factors are you using to make your decision?

- **Scenario #1:** You and a colleague (someone senior to you in the organization, but not your direct supervisor) are sent by your boss to a conference in Las Vegas. It is a three-day conference, complete with workshops, speakers, and valuable networking opportunities. The cost to your employer was significant. After diligently attending the conference events for two days, your coworker decides she is ready to have some fun in Vegas! She asks you to either join her, or stay at the conference, but not tell anyone back at the office that she did not attend the final day of the conference. What do you do?

- **Scenario #2:** You are bothered by the actions of your supervisor, who makes comments with sexual overtones, and occasionally touches you in a manner that makes you feel uncomfortable. This person seems to do this equally with everyone in your division. You have never been propositioned, though, and nothing has ever been made explicit; you think it might be all in your head. What do you do?

- **Scenario #3:** You are chosen to be a member of an interview team that will interview prospective candidates for an open position in your organization. The other three members of the team, all senior members of the organization, refuse to interview one of the candidates whose resume shows involvement in an Islamic religious organization. You suspect their resistance is rooted in discrimination, but no one said any such thing aloud. They offer no good reason for their avoidance of the candidate, but you are outvoted, and they just want to move on. What do you do?

- **Scenario #4:** You notice that your pay stub is consistently $50 per month more than it should be, based on your accepted salary offer when you started. You're afraid if you point it out now, you'll have to pay back what was mistakenly added to your check over the past 10 months. What do you do?

- **Scenario #5:** Your office mate is constantly on the phone, taking personal calls at work, and surfing websites all day long. Occasionally, she will just leave mid-day and give you a wink on her way out the door. Your shared supervisor raises concerns to you about her work output. What do you do?